always up to date

The law changes, but Nolo is always on top of it! We offer several ways to make sure you and your Nolo products are always up to date:

1 **Nolo's Legal Updater**

We'll send you an email whenever a new edition of your book is published! Sign up at **www.nolo.com/legalupdater**.

2 **Updates @ Nolo.com**

Check **www.nolo.com/update** to find recent changes in the law that affect the current edition of your book.

3 **Nolo Customer Service**

To make sure that this edition of the book is the most recent one, call us at **800-728-3555** and ask one of our friendly customer service representatives. Or find out at **www.nolo.com**.

2nd edition

Living Wills & Powers of Attorney for California

(formerly Medical Directives and
Powers of Attorney for California)

by Shae Irving, J.D.

Second Edition	NOVEMBER 2003
Editor	MARY RANDOLPH
Cover Illustration	DENIS CLIFFORD
Book Design	TERRI HEARSH
Index	THÉRÈSE SHERE
Proofreading	ROBERT WELLS
Printing	CONSOLIDATED PRINTERS, INC.

Irving, Shae.
   Living Wills and powers of attorney for California / by Shae Irving -- 2nd ed.
      p. cm.
   Includes index.
   ISBN 0-87337-993-4 (alk. paper)
   1. Right to die--Law and legislation--California--Popular works. 2.
Do-not-resuscitate--Law and legislation--California--Popular works. 3. Power of
attorney--California--Popular works. 4. Advance directives (Medical care)--California. I.
Title.

KFC619.5.R5I78 2004
344.79404'197--dc22

2003061465

For information on bulk purchases or corporate premium sales, please contact the Special Sales
Department. For academic sales or textbook adoptions, ask for Academic Sales. Call 800-955-4775 or
write to Nolo at 950 Parker Street, Berkeley, CA 94710.

Acknowledgments

Many thanks to Mary Randolph, a brilliant editor and a good friend. Thanks also to Mary, Denis Clifford, and Barbara Kate Repa for generously sharing their thoughts, ideas, and earlier work on health care directives and financial powers of attorney. This book stands on the strong foundation they built.

Finally, much gratitude to Terri Hearsh for designing the book and carefully formatting each form, to Toni Ihara for her cover design, to Robert Wells for diligent proofreading, to Andre Zivkovich for putting the forms on the CD-ROM, and to Jaleh Doane for shepherding the whole thing through production. It's a privilege and pleasure to work with these good folks.

About the Author

Shae Irving graduated from Boalt Hall School of Law at the University of California at Berkeley in 1993 and joined the editorial staff at Nolo in 1994. She is the author or co-author of several Nolo products, including the *Quicken WillMaker Plus* software. Shae is also the editor of many Nolo books, among them *Plan Your Estate* and *Nolo's Simple Will Book.*

Table of Contents

5 Help Beyond the Book

Appendixes

A How to Use the CD-ROM

B Tear-Out Forms

Index

Introduction

How to Use This Book

The purpose of this book is to make things easier on you and your family if you ever become incapacitated—that is, if you can no longer take care of yourself, personally or financially. It can also help if someone you care about is approaching incapacity and needs assistance. The forms in this book allow you to do three essential things to increase your peace of mind during a difficult time:

- state the kinds of medical treatment you do or do not want if you are no longer able to speak for yourself
- name someone to carry out those health care wishes and make other necessary medical decisions for you, and
- name someone to handle financial matters for you if you can no longer manage them on your own.

You can accomplish these tasks by completing two or three of the simple legal forms in this book.

Advance Health Care Directive. This is the official California form that permits you to state your wishes for health care and name a trusted person who will work with doctors and other health care providers on your behalf. If you like, you can also use this form to name the doctor you want to supervise your care if possible, to state your wishes about organ donation after your death, and to note what kind of body disposition and other final arrangements you would like. (See Chapter 2.)

"Living Will" or "Advance Directive"?

The news is full of talk about "living wills." That's the name commonly given to the document in which you state your preferences for health care if you are someday unable to communicate those wishes. People are usually most concerned with stating their wishes about the use of medical technology at the very end of life.

In California, a living will goes by a different name: Advance Health Care Directive. This document lets you do more than you can do in a traditional living will. You can use it to both state your health care wishes in detail and name someone to carry out those wishes and make other necessary medical decisions for you.

This book uses the term Advance Health Care Directive, not living will. But you can rest assured that the document it offers is the one you need to ensure that your wishes are clearly communicated and carefully followed.

Do Not Resuscitate (DNR) Order. Some people who do not wish to receive life-prolonging treatment when close to death may also want to prepare a DNR order. If a medical emergency occurs, this form alerts emergency medical personnel that you do not wish to receive cardiopulmonary resuscitation (CPR). (See Chapter 3.)

Durable Power of Attorney for Finances. This official California form allows you to appoint the person of your choice to manage your finances for you if someday you can no longer do so yourself. (See Chapter 4.)

This book also contains a wallet card you can use to alert others to the existence of your advance directive, and forms you can use if you ever change your mind and want to revise or revoke a document.

All of the forms in this book are legally valid in California. They are straightforward and fairly easy to complete. You probably won't need a lawyer's help. We give you detailed instructions and suggestions so that you can prepare documents that will accurately reflect your wishes and be readily accepted by others. In a few situations, however, legal advice might be helpful or necessary—so we'll tell you if it looks like your circumstances are unusual enough to warrant personalized advice from a lawyer or other expert.

All the forms are available as tear-outs (see Appendix B) and on a CD-ROM at the back of the book; you can make your documents using whichever method is more comfortable for you. After you've filled out your forms, we tell you exactly what you need to do to make them legally valid—for example, whether or not you must have your documents notarized or witnessed, and how to take care of those tasks. And we show you how to be sure the right people know about your forms, so that your documents will be readily available and honored if they're ever needed.

To get you started, Chapter 1 explains more about what incapacity is, why everyone should do at least a little bit of planning, and some important things you should think about when making your plan.

Icons Used in This Book

 Slow down and consider potential problems.

 Take advantage of an important tip.

 Go to these sources for more information about the particular issue or topic discussed in the text.

 Consider talking with a lawyer about your situation.

 Customize your forms using the CD-ROM included with this book.

The California Probate Code

Throughout this book you will see many citations to the California Probate Code. These citations look something like this: Cal. Prob. Code § 4000. The California Probate Code is the body of laws that governs the forms contained in this book—and most other things having to do with planning for incapacity and estate planning in California. The last number in the citation is important—it's the section of the code where you can find the actual law (also called a statute) supporting what we say. If you ever want to read the law itself, all you have to do is visit a law library or go online to look up the section number. Chapter 5 explains how.

Planning Ahead—An Overview

I f you're like most people, you aren't eager to spend time thinking about what would happen if you became unable to take care of yourself because of illness, an accident, or advanced age. It can be just as difficult to contemplate what would happen if a loved one, perhaps an aging parent or an ailing partner, reaches that stage. But sometimes it's impossible to avoid these issues. You may find yourself wondering: Who would pay my bills and take care of my house if I got sick? How would doctors know what kind of medical care I want to receive if I were hurt in an accident and couldn't tell them myself? Who's going to take care of Mom's finances when her Alzheimer's disease grows worse?

If you don't do at least a little bit of planning—naming someone you trust to direct your medical care and handle your finances—these personal matters could wind up in the hands of doctors or in front of courts who may know very little about what you would prefer. It's far better to spend a few hours completing the legal documents that will make your wishes clear.

As you think about your preferences for health care and property management, you may be surprised by the range of concerns that arise. In addition to practical and financial considerations, there will surely be emotional aspects to the choices you make. Your own feelings, values, and personal relationships will shape many of your decisions. For many people, making end-of-life medical decisions will also be a time for spiritual reflection and inquiry.

While this book can't address all of the practical, emotional and spiritual elements of planning for a time when you may need help with basic care, it can help you understand your options and ensure that there won't be legal complications if that time does come.

This chapter introduces the subject of incapacity and how to plan ahead for the time when help may be necessary. It explains the process and briefly describes the legal forms you will need. Chapters 2, 3, and 4 show you how to complete your forms.

You can also use this book if you are helping someone else to plan ahead and make the necessary documents. If you are using this book to help someone else, Section F of this chapter discusses some of the unique issues you may face.

A. Why You Should Plan for Incapacity

Almost every adult can benefit from some planning for incapacity. Here are a few important reasons to take the time to make at least the basic documents directing your medical care and financial management—as well as to consider some of the other planning methods discussed in Section G, below.

1. Getting the Care You Want

Making an advance directive for health care and a power of attorney for finances (the documents in this book) is the best way—and sometimes the only way—to ensure that you will get the kind of care you want. If you don't make documents directing your health care, you might receive treatment that is very different from what you would have wished. And if you don't authorize someone to oversee your finances, a court could put those matters into the hands of someone you'd never choose for the job.

It's especially important to plan ahead if your circumstances make it likely that family members won't understand your wishes, or if a court might be inclined to appoint someone other than your first choice to make decisions for you. For example, planning is essential if you are a member of an unmarried couple, straight or gay, and you want your partner to take responsibility for your health care and finances if someday you need help. Without the right legal documents, a court could choose another family member to make financial decisions on your behalf. (This is slowly changing. See "Benefits for Domestic Partners in California," below.)

It's also crucial to make a plan if you feel strongly about any of the details of your medical care or financial management. Only you know the particulars of your wishes—for example, that you never want to be placed on a respirator or that your house shouldn't be sold while you are alive, even if you can no longer live there. Writing down these finer points is the best way to prevent them from being lost.

Benefits for Domestic Partners in California

California law gives a number of benefits to couples registered as domestic partners with the Secretary of State's office. For purposes of this book, what's most important is that registered domestic partners have as much authority to make medical decisions for each other as spouses do. (Cal. Prob. Code § 4716.) And if a court must appoint someone to make medical or financial decisions on your behalf, your registered domestic partner (or someone nominated by your partner) gets the highest preference—again, the same as a spouse. (Cal. Prob. Code § 1812.)

The law requires you to register your partnership with the state to qualify for these benefits. You and your partner may register if:

- you live together
- you agree to be responsible for each other's basic living expenses for as long as your partnership lasts
- neither of you is married or the member of another currently registered domestic partnership
- you are not related by blood in a way that would prevent you from being married in California
- you are each at least 18 years old, and
- you are both capable of consenting to the domestic partnership.

In addition, you must meet one of the following requirements:

- you are of the same sex, or
- one or both of you is over the age of 62 *and* one or both of you meet the eligibility criteria for old-age insurance benefits under Title II of the Social Security Act (42 U.S.C. § 402(a)) or the eligibility requirements for benefits under Title XVI of the Social Security Act (42 U.S.C. § 1381).

For information about domestic partnership registration and the forms you need to register, visit the Secretary of State's website at www.ss.ca.gov/dpregistry or call the office at 916-653-3984.

2. Helping Those Who Care About You

Writing down your wishes now can be a great help to those close to you if you ever become unable to care for yourself. In fact, your family members and close friends are likely to look upon your planning as a minor miracle. It means that loved ones won't have to spend long, agonizing hours (and sometimes a lot of money) trying to sort out what you would want, perhaps facing disagreements and disputes among themselves as they do so. Even well-meaning family members can and do argue about decisions relating to health care and money. Especially during a stressful time, different people may sincerely and strongly disagree about what's best for you.

By stating your wishes in advance, you may not take care of any discomfort others might have about your preferences—but most people will respect what you have asked for and accept your plan. And anyone who wants to challenge your documents will probably be unsuccessful, facing a losing battle in court unless he or she can show that you were not of sound mind when you made your plan, or that you signed documents under duress or as the result of fraud.

3. Avoiding Conservatorship Proceedings

It may be easiest to understand why it's so important to plan ahead by considering in more detail what can happen if you don't.

If you have not made documents directing your health care and you become incapacitated, the doctors who take care of you will suggest what kind of medical care you should receive and turn to family members for decisions. Problems often arise when family members disagree among themselves—or when family members and partners disagree—about what treatment is proper. The most common result is that emotions run high as family members and loved ones take sides in an attempt to take care of you in the way they think best, with all involved sincerely believing they have your best interest at heart.

In the most complicated scenarios, these battles over medical care wind up in court. If that happens, a judge, who usually has little medical knowledge and no familiarity with you, is called upon to decide the future of your treatment, usually by giving one person power to make health care decisions for you. (This person is called a "conservator.") Such battles are costly, time consuming, and painful to those involved—and they are unnecessary if you have the foresight to use a formal document to express your wishes for your health care.

If you don't make a document naming someone to manage your finances, similar battles may ensue. Without the necessary document, your relatives or other loved ones will have to ask a judge to name a conservator to manage your finances.

The upshot of all this is that, without a couple of simple legal documents prepared in advance, a court may have to appoint a conservator to take care of your medical care, finances, or both. Conservatorship proceedings can be complicated, expensive, and embarrassing. Your loved ones must ask the court to rule that you cannot take care of yourself—a public airing of a very private matter. Court proceedings are matters of public record; in some places, a notice may even be published in a local newspaper. If relatives fight over who is to be the conservator, the proceedings will surely become even more disagreeable, sometimes downright nasty. And all of this causes costs to mount up, especially if lawyers must be hired.

What's more, if a conservator is appointed to handle your finances, conservatorship proceedings are just the beginning of court involvement. Often a conservator of property must:

- post a bond—a kind of insurance policy that pays if the conservator steals or misuses property
- prepare (or hire a lawyer to prepare) detailed reports and periodically file them with the court
- get court approval for certain transactions, such as selling real estate or making slightly risky investments.

Conservators in charge of your personal care—including health care decisions—may be required to report to a court as well.

You can see why it's usually far less burdensome to take the time to prepare an advance directive and a power of attorney. There are only a very few situations in which a conservatorship might actually be desirable; these are discussed in Sections B1 (for health care) and C2 (for finances), below.

B. Using Medical Directives

Let's take a brief look at the two health care documents you can make with this book.

1. Advance Health Care Directive

In California, the document you use to direct your health care is called an Advance Health Care Directive. California's advance directive form permits you to do several important things.

Name someone to carry out your health care wishes and make other medical decisions for you. The first part of the advance directive form is called a "durable power of attorney for health care." A power of attorney is simply a legal document that you use to name someone to make decisions for you or take action on your behalf. The word "attorney" here means anyone authorized to act for you; that person definitely doesn't have to be a lawyer.

A power of attorney is considered "durable" if it stays in effect even after you are incapacitated. Powers of attorney that aren't durable are not valid if you are no longer able to make your own decisions.

You use this part of the form, the durable power of attorney, to name the person who will make sure your health care preferences are honored and who will make any other necessary medical decisions for you. This person is called your agent, or your health care agent. Most people name their spouse, partner, or a grown child as agent. It's best to appoint just one agent and name a backup in case that person is unable to serve. The form allows you to name up to two alternate agents.

The advance directive gives your agent broad authority to make health care decisions on your behalf, though if you choose, you can limit your agent's authority when you complete your document. Appointing your agent and defining the powers you want to grant is discussed in detail in Chapter 2, Section B.

State your health care wishes. You can state your preferences for medical treatment in as little or as much detail as you like. For example, you can indicate whether or not you want to receive life-prolonging treatment—a respirator, CPR, surgery, and the like—if you are close to death from a terminal illness, in a permanent coma, or if your agent (after consulting with your doctor) determines that treatment would be more likely to put you at risk than to help you. You can choose from general statements about your wishes, or you can write out as many specifics as you like about the kinds of treatments you do or do not wish to receive under various circumstances. We guide you through your options in Chapter 2, Section C, Part 2, providing samples you can use if you want to include detailed wishes in your form.

Specify whether you wish to donate organs, tissues, or body parts after your death. If you want to donate any of your organs or body parts after death, the advance directive form contains a place for you to say so. This is discussed in Chapter 2, Section C, Part 3.

Name the primary physician who will be responsible for your care. If you have an established relationship with a doctor whom you trust, you may want to specify that this doctor supervise your care, working with your health care agent. See Chapter 2, Section C, Part 4.

When You Might Not Want to Appoint an Agent for Health Care

It's never a bad idea to write out your health care wishes. Doing so can only help you get the kind of treatment you want. There is one circumstance, however, in which it may not be wise to appoint a health care agent. You shouldn't do it if you don't know anyone that you trust with the job. Your agent functions without court supervision (that's the point of naming one), so it's critical that you choose someone who can understand your wishes and is willing and able to be your advocate if necessary. (More on this in Chapter 2, Section B4.) If you don't know anyone who fits this bill, it's usually better to let a court appoint a conservator for you if necessary. That way, your conservator must report to a judge who can be certain that the conservator is acting in your best interests.

Unless you indicate otherwise, your advance directive becomes effective only if your doctor determines that you are incapacitated and unable to communicate your wishes for care. If you prefer, however, you can allow your health care agent—not a doctor—to decide when to put your document into effect. See Chapter 2, Section A2.

2. Do Not Resuscitate (DNR) Order

If, in your advance directive, you state that you do not wish to receive life-sustaining treatment; you may also want to consider preparing a simple form called a Prehospital Do Not Resuscitate (DNR) Order. (In California, this is sometimes known as a "Request to Forgo Resuscitative Measures," but we call it by its less cumbersome and more common name.)

A prehospital DNR order is used for the specific and limited purpose of alerting emergency medical personnel to the fact that you do not wish to receive cardiopulmonary resuscitation (CPR) in the event of a medical emergency. This means that if you are anywhere other than in the hospital—for example, at home or outside somewhere—and you collapse, the paramedics who respond to the emergency call will not attempt to restart your heart or your breathing. If you are already in the hospital, you can ask your doctor to place a DNR order in your medical record; there's no need to create a separate form.

DNR orders are sometimes used by those who:

- have a terminal illness
- are at increased risk for cardiac or respiratory arrest, or
- oppose the use of CPR under any circumstances.

If you know you don't want to receive CPR in an emergency, preparing a DNR order is a good idea. If you don't have one, emergency medical personnel will do all they can to save your life, including administering CPR. Even if you've prepared an advance directive stating that you don't wish to receive CPR, emergency teams won't likely know of its existence.

In addition to preparing the DNR form, you will want to get a MedicAlert bracelet or medallion to wear so that your wishes will be obvious to medical personnel. We explain how to complete the form and obtain a medallion in Chapter 3.

C. Using a Durable Power of Attorney for Finances

A durable power of attorney for finances allows you to name someone to take care of your financial matters if you become incapacitated and can't handle them yourself. ("Durable" simply means that the document stays in effect after you are incapacitated.) You can make the document effective immediately, if you need or want help right away. Or you can make what's known as a "springing" durable power of attorney—a document that doesn't take effect unless and until you become incapacitated.

The trusted person you name—again, called your "agent"—will have whatever financial powers you grant to him or her. You can authorize your agent to pay bills (with your assets), make bank deposits, claim government benefits, manage your investments, and handle many other financial matters. (See Chapter 4, Section B1, for more on an agent's authority.)

As you begin thinking about appointing an agent, keep in mind that it's usually best to name just one person, and that it's wise to name the same person to take care of your finances that you named to make health care decisions for you. If that's not possible, it's critical that you name two people who can work well together. (See Chapter 4, Section B4, for help choosing your agent.)

Most people with property or an income can benefit from making a durable power of attorney for finances. But it's not the right document in every situation. Following are some answers to common questions about when you should—and shouldn't— rely on a durable power of attorney for finances.

1. Do You Need a Durable Power of Attorney?

You may not think that you need a durable power of attorney for finances (DPAF) if you're married, or if you've put most of your property into a living trust or hold it in joint tenancy. But the truth is that in all of these situations, a durable power of attorney can make life much easier for your family if you become incapacitated.

a. If You Are Married

Don't assume that your spouse will automatically be able to manage your finances if you can't. Your spouse does have some authority over property you own together—for example, to pay bills from a joint bank account or sell stock in a joint brokerage account. There are significant limits, however, on your spouse's right to sell property owned by both of you. For example, both spouses must agree to the sale of co-owned real estate or cars. Because an incapacitated spouse can't consent to such a sale, the other spouse's hands are tied.

And when it comes to property that belongs only to you, your spouse has no legal authority. You must use a durable power of attorney to give your spouse authority over your property.

b. If You Have a Living Trust

If you've made a revocable living trust, you know that its primary purpose is to avoid probate. But the trust can also be useful if you become incapable of taking care of your financial affairs. That's because the person who will distribute trust property after your death (called the successor trustee) can also, in most cases, take over management of the trust property if you become incapacitated. Usually, the trust document gives the successor trustee authority to manage all property in the trust and to use it for your needs.

However, the successor trustee has no authority over property not held in trust. Most people transfer into a living trust assets that are expensive to probate, such as real estate and valuable securities, but few people hold all their property in a living trust. So although it's helpful, a living trust isn't a complete substitute for a durable power of attorney for finances.

c. If You Own Joint Tenancy Property

Joint tenancy is a way that more than one person can own property together. The most notable feature of joint tenancy is that when one owner dies, the other owners automatically inherit the deceased person's share of the property. But if you become incapacitated, the other owners have very limited authority over your share of the joint tenancy property. For example, if you and someone else own a bank account in joint tenancy and one of you becomes incapacitated, the other owner is legally entitled t use the funds. The healthy joint tenant can take car of the financial needs of the incapacitated perso simply by paying bills from the joint account. But th other account owner has no legal right to endors checks made out to the incapacitated person. I practice, it might be possible—if not technicall legal—to get an incapacitated person's checks into joint account by stamping them "For Deposit Only, but that's not the easiest way to handle things

Matters get even more complicated with othe kinds of joint tenancy property. Real estate is a

good example. If one owner becomes incapacitated, the other has no legal authority to sell or refinance the incapacitated owner's share.

By contrast, with a durable power of attorney, you can give your agent authority over your share of joint tenancy property, including real estate and bank accounts.

2. When You Shouldn't Rely on a Durable Power of Attorney

As discussed in Section A3, above, the expense and intrusion of a conservatorship are rarely desirable. In a few situations, however, special concerns make a conservatorship preferable to giving someone authority under a durable power of attorney.

a. You Want Court Supervision of Your Finances

If you can't think of someone you trust enough to appoint as your agent, with broad authority over your property and finances, don't create a durable power of attorney for finances. A conservatorship, with the built-in safeguard of court supervision, is worth the extra cost and trouble.

b. You Fear Family Fights

A durable power of attorney is a readily accepted and powerful legal document. Once you've finalized yours, anyone who wants to challenge your plans for financial management will face a tough, and probably losing, battle in court. But if you expect that family members will challenge your document or make continual trouble for your agent, a conservatorship may be preferable. Your relatives may still fight, but at least the court will be there to keep an eye on your welfare and your property.

 If you're undecided. If you expect family fights and feel uncomfortable making a durable power of attorney for finances, you may want to talk with a knowledgeable lawyer. An expert who's experienced in these matters can help you weigh your concerns and options, and help you decide whether a durable power of attorney is the best choice for you.

D. The Mental Capacity Requirement

To make a health care directive or power of attorney for finances, you must be of sound mind. In other words, you cannot make valid documents if you are already incapacitated.

In terms of your medical care, you are of sound mind as long as you can understand the nature and consequences of your health care choices (including significant benefits, risks, and alternatives) and communicate your wishes for care.

For money matters, your mental capacity is determined by a similar standard. You are mentally competent as long as you can understand the rights, responsibilities, risks, or benefits involved in your financial decisions, and the potential consequences of what you decide.

If you have physical disabilities but are otherwise able to understand your health care and financial choices, your documents will be perfectly valid.

When you sign a document, no one makes a determination about your mental state. The issue will come up later only if someone goes to court and challenges the document, claiming that you weren't of sound mind when you signed it. That kind of lawsuit is very rare.

Even in the highly unlikely event of a court hearing, the competency requirement is not difficult to satisfy. If you understood what you were doing when you signed your medical directive or power of attorney, that's enough. To make this determination, a judge would probably question those who knew you well at the time you made your document. There would be no general inquiry into your life. It wouldn't matter, for example, that you were occasionally forgetful or absentminded around the time when you signed your power of attorney document or health care directive.

 Heading off problems. If you think someone is likely to go to court and challenge your documents or claim that you were coerced into signing them, see a good estate planning lawyer. The lawyer can review the documents you create yourself or draw up some documents for you. (This is not necessary in most circumstances, as discussed in the next section.) An experienced lawyer can also answer any questions you have about your documents directing medical care and financial management—and about other estate planning documents as well. For example, you may also be expecting challenges to your will or a trust. You can talk with a lawyer about all of these issues. Your attorney can also testify about your mental competency, should the need arise.

E. Will You Need a Lawyer?

You can probably prepare the documents in this book without any help from lawyer. In fact, the California advance directive and power of attorney forms are designed so that people can complete them easily, without professional assistance. If, however, you have specific questions or unusual circumstances —for example, unusually contentious family members or a very large amount of property—you may need legal advice. As you read this book, you'll be alerted to circumstances where you may run into trouble or benefit from a lawyer's help. If you do need to see a lawyer, the information in Chapter 5 can help you find a good one.

F. If a Loved One Needs Help

Many people find themselves in the painful position of seeing a family member or close friend lose the ability to make sound medical and financial decisions. In addition to the grief of watching a loved one's condition deteriorate, a caretaker's situation can be made more difficult if the person in need of help denies—or is oblivious to—worsening physical or mental health.

If the person you're caring for is of sound mind (see Section D, above) and receptive to the idea of setting out medical wishes and naming someone to watch over medical and financial decisions, that makes things much easier. You can use this book to explain the process, answer questions, and help prepare and finalize the right documents. But if you think someone who needs help will resist your efforts, you need to carefully consider the way you approach the subject.

For some stubborn folks, it may be enough to explain why planning is important. Some people may be moved by a request to plan ahead because it will relieve much anxiety and pressure for you and the others who care about them, even if they don't much care what happens or who makes decisions for them. Others may be more inclined to make health care and financial documents if they understand that doing so is the best way for them to stay in control of their lives, because whomever they name must follow their instructions in every way possible. Of course, when you talk with anyone who's struggling with increasing frailty, you will have to tread very gently around issues of deteriorating mental or physical abilities, perhaps underscoring that planning is a good thing for *anybody* to do, just in case it's necessary someday.

All that said, it's just as important to remember that legally you can't—and you shouldn't—try to force someone to follow a certain course just because you think it's best. If you strong-arm or coerce someone into making documents and those documents are later challenged in court, you could find yourself in a lot of legal trouble. The same goes for faking signatures on any legal documents. Don't do it. If your loved one doesn't want to cooperate and you eventually have to ask a court for control over his or her affairs, that may be difficult, but it's much better than being charged with fraud or forgery. Under California law, you could be forced to pay at least $10,000 if a court finds you guilty of such behavior. (Cal. Prob. Code § 4742(b).)

If it's too late to plan. As discussed in Section D, above, a person must be of sound mind to make the documents in this book. If a family member is already incapacitated and you need to ask a court to name a conservator, Nolo's *Conservatorship Book for California*, by Lisa Goldoftas and Elizabeth A. Hendrickson, provides you with everything you need to obtain a legal conservatorship in California without a lawyer.

Getting support. The following resources may help you cope with some of the stresses of caregiving:

The 36-Hour Day, by Nancy L. Mac and Peter V. Rabins, M.D., is a comprehensive guide to caring for people with Alzheimer's disease, as well as other types of dementia and memory loss.

The Family Caregiver Alliance, 690 Market Street, Suite 600, San Francisco, CA 94104, 415-434-3388, is a support organization and information clearinghouse for families and friends providing care for someone who is incapacitated. You can browse their offerings on the Web at www.caregiver.org.

The National Alzheimer's Association provides resources and support for people caring for a loved one with Alzheimer's disease. You can find lots of free information on the organization's website at www.alz.org. You can also contact them by mail or phone: 225 North Michigan Avenue, Suite 1700, Chicago, IL 60601-7633, 800-272-3900.

Children of Aging Parents is a nonprofit organization that provides information, referrals, and support to caregivers. Visit its website at www.caps4caregivers.org or call 800-227-7294.

G. Other Important Issues to Consider

Making the most important documents in this book —the advance health care directive and the durable power of attorney for finances—will take you a long way in your planning. Once you've completed them, you can be confident that someone you trust will be on hand to take care of you, personally and financially. But there are a few other things you should consider when thinking ahead. Here is a brief look at the most important of them.

1. Long-Term Care

Someday, you or a close family member may need some kind of long-term care. A significant number of older people, even if they remain basically healthy, develop physical or mental frailties or impairments that at some point prevent them from living independent lives.

"Long-term care" may be defined in many ways, but essentially it means regular assistance with medical care or personal needs—for example, eating, dressing, bathing, or moving around—provided by someone other than a family member. There are many types of long-term care available these days, ranging from part-time home care, to adult day care, to independent living and assisted living residential communities, to nursing facilities. Some long-term care is temporary—for example, if you're recovering from a broken hip or a stroke. In other cases, permanent care is necessary.

The need for temporary or permanent care raises a number of difficult questions:

- What kind of care is needed?
- Who will provide it?
- Where will it be provided?
- How much will it cost?
- Who will pay for it?

If you appoint an agent for health care and finances and you do nothing else, you won't be left out in the cold when it comes to long-term care. Your agent will most likely be the one to find answers to these questions and try to get you the care you need. You can make the job much easier by thinking about, talking about, and planning for potential needs ahead of time. Discussing your preferences and making a plan for financing necessary care—including an evaluation of long-term care insurance and potentially available government benefits—will save your agent and other family members a lot of time, trouble, and money down the road.

Help with long-term care decisions. *Choose the Right Long-Term Care: Home Care, Assisted Living & Nursing Homes*, by Joseph L. Matthews (Nolo), can help you understand the many alternatives to nursing facilities and show you how to fit the care you need to the funds you have available. Topics covered include arranging in-home care, finding a non-nursing facility residence, choosing a nursing home, getting the most out of Medicare and other benefit programs, evaluating long-term care insurance, protecting your assets when the costs of care start to mount, and other important matters.

Who Decides Where You Will Live?

If you become incapacitated and are unable to continue living at home, you may wonder who will make the decision about where you will live. California law permits you to use your durable power of attorney for health care to give your health care agent the authority to decide where you will reside. (Cal. Prob. Code § 4671.) However, you should remember that it's your agent for *finances* who will have the authority to pay for the costs of your living arrangements. This brings up an important point, discussed in both Chapters 2 and 4: It's almost always best to name the same person as your agent for health care and finances. If you can't name just one person for some reason, it's critical that you name two people who can work well together and make decisions as a team.

In any case, it's a very good idea to spend some time thinking about where you would want to live if you could no longer live at home. If you want to remain at home or with relatives as long as possible, taking advantage of the benefits of in-home care—or if you have a care facility in mind—you should speak to your health care agent, agent for finances, and close family and friends about your wishes. This will help them make the best decision for you. You may even want to note these wishes in your advance health care directive. (See Chapter 2, Section C, Part 1.) If your agents or family members ever have a bad squabble over your living arrangements and wind up in court (not likely, but it has happened), your notes will help the judge understand your preferences.

2. Arranging Care for Young Children

You can't use a power of attorney to give anyone authority to care for your minor children (those under 18) if you become incapacitated. In your durable power of attorney for finances, you can give your agent the authority to pay for the children's needs out of your assets—but the agent's power under the document stops there. If you become incapacitated, your children's other parent will be responsible for taking care of them. If the other parent is not available, a court will appoint some-one—a close family member, if possible—to do it.

In California, if you have been diagnosed with a terminal illness, you may ask a court to nominate another person as a "joint guardian" along with you. (Cal. Prob. Code § 2105(f).) This process is intended to alleviate some of the emotional stress and disruption kids suffer when a parent becomes seriously ill and later dies. The joint guardian has the same rights and responsibilities for your child as you do. The court can't appoint a joint guardian over the ob-jection of your child's other parent unless it first finds that granting custody to the other parent would be bad for the child.

Under circumstances other than terminal illness, to name a guardian who will care for your young children if you die, you should write a will (see below). The court will give strong weight to your recommendation when appointing the guardian. (If a court appoints a joint guardian when you are ter-minally ill, there is no need to name a guardian in your will. The person appointed by the court will continue to care for your children after you die.)

3. Leaving Your Property

If you're thinking about end-of-life issues, you'll probably want to make some decisions about who will receive your property when you die. You can use a will, living trust, or other legal transfer method (such as joint tenancy ownership) to carry out your wishes. Along with deciding how property will be distributed, you may want to explore strategies for avoiding probate—the time-consuming and often wasteful court proceedings after death. And if you're very wealthy, you will probably want to explore methods of eliminating or reducing estate taxes.

The easiest thing to do is to draw up a simple will. This is important if you own any property that matters to you, so that it will be passed on as you wish. And, as mentioned above, it's critical if you have kids under 18. People with young children should write a will to nominate a guardian who will raise their children if they can't, and they should make a plan for how the children's property will be managed. (Minors, by law, can't control any signifi-cant amount of property they own.)

Below you'll find a list of resources from Nolo that can help you with wills, trusts, and other as-pects of what lawyers call "estate planning."

4. Winding Up Your Affairs After Death

With one important exception, you can't give an agent the power to handle tasks after your death, such as paying your debts or transferring property to the people who inherit it. The exception is this: Your agent for health care is permitted to handle the disposition of your body after your death, including donating organs, authorizing an autopsy, and handling funeral arrangements, unless you say otherwise in your advance health care directive. (See Chapter 2, Section C, Part 1.)

If you want an agent to have authority to wind up the rest of your affairs after death, use your will to name that person as your executor. If you also plan to avoid probate, you may want to prepare a living trust and name that person as your successor trustee—the person who will manage and distribute trust property after your death.

Making Final Arrangements

Do your family members know what kind of body disposition and memorial ceremonies you want after your death? If they don't, it may be very difficult for them to make these decisions at a time when they are already feeling overwhelmed. Planning in this area can also help save some money. Without it, funeral and related costs can be very expensive.

Your advance health care directive is a fine place to make some notes about the final arrangements that you want. If you have the time and the inclination, you can write a statement or a letter setting out your wishes and attach it to your advance directive. This way, your survivors will have your wishes at hand when the time comes. To learn more about how to do this, see Chapter 2, Section C, Part 1.

More information about estate planning. Nolo offers many tools designed to help you with basic estate planning tasks. You may want to start by visiting Nolo's website at www.nolo.com, where you'll find lots of helpful (and free) information about estate planning in our legal encyclopedia.

Quicken WillMaker Plus (software for Windows) allows you to prepare a comprehensive will and living trust using your computer. It also enables you to prepare a final arrangements document and many other useful legal forms.

Plan Your Estate, by Denis Clifford and Cora Jordan, offers in-depth coverage of all significant elements of estate planning, from simple wills to probate avoidance and complex tax-saving trusts.

Estate Planning Basics, by Denis Clifford, is a short course in estate planning, providing straightforward explanations that help you learn just what you need to know to make your plan.

Nolo's Simple Will Book, by Denis Clifford, shows you how to prepare a will that covers your needs, including basic trusts for minor children. Will forms are available as tear-outs or on a CD-ROM included with the book.

The Quick & Legal Will Book, by Denis Clifford, enables you to efficiently prepare a basic will.

Make Your Own Living Trust, by Denis Clifford, provides a complete explanation of how to prepare a living trust. The book contains forms (tear-out and on CD-ROM) allowing you to create a probate avoidance living trust and, for married couples, a tax-saving "AB" trust.

8 Ways to Avoid Probate, by Mary Randolph, offers a thorough discussion of all the major ways to avoid probate by transferring property at death outside of a will.

How to Probate an Estate in California, by Julia Nissley, walks you step-by-step through the process of probating an estate in California, with lots of helpful information for executors. ■

Advance Health Care Directives

To ensure that your preferences for medical care will be understood and followed, you will want to prepare an Advance Health Care Directive. As described in Chapter 1, with a California advance directive you can:

- write out specific instructions that describe the medical care you do or do not want if you can no longer express your wishes, and
- name someone you trust to supervise your wishes and direct your health care in any situations that you don't cover in your written instructions.

If you like, you can also use your advance directive to name the primary physician whom you want to be responsible for your care, and you can state whether you wish to donate any organs or body parts after your death.

A. How Advance Directives Work

You have a constitutional right to control your own medical care. The U.S. Supreme Court has said that "clear and convincing" evidence of an individual's wishes about medical care should be followed—even if they conflict with the wishes of close family members. (*Cruzan v. Director, Missouri Dept. of Health*, 497 U.S. 261 (1990).) A doctor who receives a properly signed and witnessed or notarized advance directive has a duty either to honor its instructions, or to make sure the patient is transferred to the care of another doctor who will honor them.

When you make your advance directive, you can say as much or as little as you wish about the kind of health care you want to receive. Some people don't say anything at all; they just use their advance directive to name an agent who will make all medical decisions for them if they become incapacitated. For example, you can leave it to your agent to direct all of your medical care, including decisions about whether or not you would receive life-prolonging treatment if you were ever close to death from a terminal illness or in a permanent coma. But if you want to control your own health care to the greatest possible extent, you can write out very detailed instructions about the kind of care you want (we show you how in Section C, Part 2) and name someone to oversee and enforce your directions.

Before you jump into preparing your advance directive, however, it's smart to understand some basic facts about the document. This section explains:

- who can make an advance directive
- when your advance directive takes effect
- the duty of medical personnel to honor your directive, and
- when your advance directive ends.

1. Who Can Make an Advance Directive

You must be at least 18 years old to make a valid document directing your health care. You must also be of sound mind—that is, able to understand what the document means, what it contains, and how it works. For a more detailed discussion of this requirement, see Chapter 1, Section D.

2. When Your Advance Directive Takes Effect

Unless you specify otherwise, your advance directive will take effect only if your primary physician someday determines that you lack the ability, or capacity, to make your own health care decisions. (Cal. Prob. Code § 4701.) Lacking capacity means that:

- you can't understand the nature and consequences of the health care choices that are available to you (including significant benefits, risks, and alternatives), and
- you are unable to communicate your own wishes for care, either orally, in writing, or through gestures. (Cal. Prob. Code § 4609.)

Practically speaking, this means that if you are so ill or injured that you cannot express your health care wishes in any way, your documents will spring immediately into effect. If, however, there is some question about your ability to understand your treatment choices and communicate clearly, your doctor will decide whether it is time for your advance directive to become operative.

If you want to give your agent authority to manage your health care immediately, however, you have that option. All you have to do is check a box on your advance directive form that makes your agent's authority effective right away. You may prefer to make an immediately effective directive for any of several reasons, including:

Taking quick action. Your agent can put your document into effect as soon as he or she feels that you have lost the ability to make your own medical decisions. The agent will be able to make decisions for you without first having a doctor confirm that you are incapacitated. This may be particularly important if you are not under the care of a doctor with whom you have an established, trusting relationship.

Keeping control in the hands of your agent. You may feel that your agent is the best person to decide that you can no longer direct your own medical care. If so, you may not need to require the statement of a doctor.

Asking your agent to step in early. If you make your document effective right away, your agent can start making decisions for you whenever you decide that's what you want, even if you still have the capacity to make your own choices. If illness, exhaustion, or any other circumstances have left you feeling that you'd like someone you trust to deal with your doctors and make treatment choices for you, making an immediately effective document gives you that flexibility.

Making your document effective immediately will *not* give your agent the authority to override what you want in terms of treatment; you will always be able to dictate your own medical care if you have the ability to do so. And remember that even when you are no longer capable of making your own decisions, your agent must act in your best interests and try diligently to follow any health care wishes you've expressed in your advance directive or otherwise. (See Section C, Part 2, below.)

3. Duty of Medical Personnel to Honor Your Advance Directive

Health care providers are generally required to comply with the wishes you set out in your advance directive, and to honor your agent's authority as long as the agent's directions are a reasonable interpretation of your wishes. (Cal. Prob. Code § 4733(a).) In some situations, however, a health care provider is permitted to reject a health care decision made by you or your agent. This is true when:

- the decision goes against the conscience of the individual health care provider (Cal. Prob. Code § 4734(a))
- the decision goes against a policy of a health care institution that is based on reasons of conscience, and that policy is promptly communicated to you or your agent (Cal. Prob. Code § 4734(b)), or
- the decision would lead to medically ineffective health care or health care that violates generally accepted health care standards applied by the health care provider or institution (Cal. Prob. Code § 4735).

But this doesn't mean that your advance directive can be ignored. A health care provider who refuses to comply with your wishes or the instructions of your agent must promptly inform you or your agent. If you or your agent wishes, the provider must immediately take steps to transfer you to another provider or institution that will honor your directive. The health care provider must continue to care for you until the transfer is complete. (Cal. Prob. Code § 4736.)

EXAMPLE: Angie is a diabetic with serious kidney problems. She feels strongly that if she is close to death or in a permanent coma, she doesn't wish to receive any more life-sustaining treatment, including kidney dialysis or artificially administered food and water—and she prepares an advance health care directive saying so. When her condition suddenly worsens, she falls into a coma from which the doctors at the local hospital don't believe she will recover.

When her agent seeks to enforce her health care wishes and discontinue life-prolonging care, the doctor in charge of her case balks, feeling especially uncomfortable about withholding nutritional fluids. But because the hospital itself does not have a policy against withholding these types of treatments, Angie's agent is able to transfer her case to another doctor who agrees to follow her directions.

If a health care provider improperly refuses to honor your wishes, your agent or any other concerned person can seek help from a court. A judge can compel the health care provider to comply with your instructions and recognize the authority of your agent. (Cal. Prob. Code § 4766(e).)

A health care provider who intentionally violates the laws discussed in this section may be legally liable for damages. Under California law, you could sue the provider for at least $2,500 and the cost of your attorney's fees. (Cal. Prob. Code § 4742.)

4. When Your Advance Directive Ends

Your written wishes for health care remain effective as long as you are alive, unless you specifically revoke your advance directive or a court steps in. Court involvement is very rare.

a. You Revoke Your Document

You can change or revoke your advance directive at any time, as long as you are of sound mind. We explain how in Section E, below.

How Pregnancy May Affect Your Advance Directive

There is one situation in which your specific directions about health care might be challenged or ignored completely: when you are pregnant. While California law does not specifically limit the effect of your advance directive if you are pregnant, if you may become pregnant it's a good idea to explicitly state what you want if your advance directive goes into effect while you are carrying a child. You can choose that your documents:

- be given no effect during pregnancy, or
- be carried out as written.

We show you how to do this in Section C, Part 2(9)c, *Directing Health Care for Different Situations*, below.

If you specify the health care wishes in your advance directive be given no effect, your agent or health care providers will have the discretion to decide what care is appropriate. They are most likely to administer whatever life-prolonging procedures are available—particularly if the fetus is at least four or five months old, potentially viable, and unharmed by your condition.

If you choose that your health care directions be carried out as written if you are pregnant, you may meet some resistance from doctors and hospitals. This is particularly true if you direct that life-prolonging treatment, pain medication, or food and water should be withheld. And you are more apt to run into resistance the more advanced your pregnancy becomes. If you are into the second trimester—the fourth through sixth months—doctors are likely to administer all medical care they deem necessary to keep you and the fetus alive.

By the third trimester of a pregnancy—the seventh through ninth months—it may be practically impossible to dictate that doctors withhold life-prolonging medical care. And doctors who balk at enforcing your contrary wishes have some legal support for ignoring you and administering all available care. Doctors can argue that while individuals may have the right to direct their own health care, they have no right to direct that care for another living being, arguably—under the U.S. Supreme Court's decision in *Roe v. Wade*, 401 U.S. 113 (1973)—a fetus six months old or older.

b. A Court Invalidates Your Document

California law sensibly recognizes that a court is normally not the right place to make health care decisions. (Cal. Prob. Code § 4650.) However, if your health care is the subject of a dispute and someone questions the validity of your advance directive, the matter may end up before a judge.

If someone doubts that you had the mental capacity to prepare a legally valid advance directive, that person can ask a court to invalidate your document. (See Cal. Prob. Code §§ 4765, 4766.) Such lawsuits are rare, but they do sometimes occur. The burden of proving that you were not of sound mind when you made your advance directive falls on the person who challenges the validity of your document. The law presumes that you had the mental capacity to make your advance directive. (Cal. Prob. Code § 4657.)

It is also possible that a court could invalidate your document if it wasn't properly witnessed or notarized (for more information about these requirements, see Section C, Part 5, below). If this happens, however, it is still likely that any wishes for health care you set out in the document will be followed—as long as they are clearly expressed and you were of sound mind when you wrote them down. In the famous *Cruzan* case, the U.S. Supreme Court said that any strong evidence of someone's wishes for care should be honored: your directions won't be ignored simply because of a technical error.

c. A Court Revokes Your Agent's Authority

If, after your document takes effect, someone believes that your agent is not acting according to your wishes or in your best interests, the concerned person can go to court and ask for an investigation of your agent's behavior.

If a court finds that your agent is acting improperly and revokes his or her authority, the job will go first to an alternate agent you named in your advance directive. If there is no available alternate (or if the court invalidates your entire document for one of the reasons discussed in Subsection b, above) a conservator will be appointed to make health care decisions for you. When naming a conservator, a court will consider the following people, in this order:

- your spouse or registered domestic partner
- an adult child
- a parent, or
- a sibling.

If one of the people on this list doesn't want to take the job of conservator, that person has the power to nominate someone else to take the position before the court moves on to the next person on the priority list. (Cal. Prob. Code § 1812.)

d. You Get a Divorce

Getting divorced has no effect on your written directions for health care. But if you named your spouse as your health care agent, his or her authority is automatically revoked when the divorce is final. (Cal. Prob. Code § 4697.) If you named an alternate agent in your advance directive, that person will take over.

If you get a divorce before your advance directive takes effect, it's wise to eliminate confusion by starting over. Even if you named an alternate, make a new document and name someone else as your agent.

If you are a member of a registered domestic partnership and you terminate that partnership, the law doesn't automatically revoke your partner's authority under an advance directive. Be sure to revise your document if you want to name a new health care agent.

e. After Your Death

Your advance directive remains effective after your death only for some very limited purposes. Your agent can supervise the disposition of your body, including authorizing an autopsy or organ donation, unless you specifically withheld these powers when you made your advance directive. (See Section C, Part 1, below.)

B. About Your Health Care Agent

One of the most important benefits of making an advance health care directive is that you get to choose someone to supervise your medical care if you are unable to do so yourself. This person is usually called your agent, but occasionally goes by "attorney-in-fact."

You can give your agent a great deal of control over your medical decisions or very little. How much authority you grant is entirely up to you. But it's almost always a good idea to name an agent, even if that person will be charged only with enforcing the detailed health care wishes you express in your advance directive. Your agent can make sure medical personnel know of your preferences, lobby on your behalf to get them enforced, and if necessary, go to court to be sure you get the kind of care you want.

If you don't name an agent to supervise your care, health care providers may not follow your wishes as diligently as they would if an agent were present. And without an agent, if doctors have questions about the kind of care you should receive, they will turn to your close family members for guidance. This will probably be fine if the person they ask is the same person you would have named as your agent—your spouse, say, or one of your grown children—and no one else who is close to you strongly disagrees with what they decide. But if your loved ones disagree about your care, they may have to ask a court to obtain the authority to make health care decisions for you or to enforce the wishes you've expressed. You can prevent these difficulties by using your advance directive to name a trusted person to represent you.

EXAMPLE: A California case illustrates the vital importance of making an advance directive and naming a health care agent. Robert Wendland was in his mid-thirties when he was severely injured in a car accident. He was in a coma for more than a year before he awakened into a state that some doctors have described as "minimally conscious." Although awake, he was severely brain-damaged and paralyzed on his right side. Six months after Robert came out of the coma, his wife Rose, who had been named Robert's conservator, decided to withhold food and fluids, saying that Robert had earlier told her and other family members that he wouldn't want to live in a state of total dependence. Robert had not, however, prepared an advance directive. Robert's doctors supported Rose's decision. However, when Robert's mother and sister learned of Rose's plans, they went to court and obtained a temporary restraining order to stop her, asserting that Robert would have wanted to be kept alive. Thus began a bitter family fight, with both sides claiming they knew what was best for Robert and battling to be named his permanent conservator. Eight years after Robert's accident, the family was still fighting.

Robert died of pneumonia in July of 2001; a month later, the Supreme Court of California ruled that conservators cannot terminate life support for conscious—though severely disabled—people without clear and convincing evidence of their wishes. (*Conservatorship of Wendland*, 110 Cal. Rptr. 2d 412 (Cal. 2001).)

1. Your Agent's Powers

As mentioned just above, you can give your agent as much or as little power as feels comfortable to you. Most people give their agent comprehensive power to supervise their care. Recognizing this, California's advance directive form gives the person you name the power to make all health care decisions for you unless you specifically limit his or her authority in the document. Unless you expressly restrict your agent's authority, your agent will have the power to:

- consent or refuse consent to any medical treatment that affects your physical or mental health, with a few exceptions discussed in the next section
- hire or fire medical personnel and make decisions about the best medical facilities for you
- approve or disapprove diagnostic tests, surgical procedures, or medications
- direct the provision, withholding, or withdrawal of artificial nutrition and hydration, and all other forms of life-sustaining medical care, including cardiopulmonary resuscitation (CPR), and
- make anatomical gifts, authorize an autopsy, and direct the disposition of your body after death.

Again, keep in mind that as long as you are able to understand and communicate your own wishes, your agent cannot override what you want. Your agent steps in only if you can no longer manage on your own.

Of course, if you also use your advance directive to specify what type of care you want to receive, your agent is legally bound to follow your wishes, as are medical care providers. (See Sections A3 and B3.) And you can restrict your agent's authority even further if you wish, by stating that his or her authority is strictly limited to enforcing whatever wishes you express. We show you how to place restrictions on your agent's authority in Section C, Part 1, below.

2. What Your Health Care Agent Can't Do

California law does not permit an agent to make certain medical decisions for you. Your agent may not:

- place you in a mental health facility (Cal. Prob. Code § 4652(a))
- authorize extreme psychiatric treatments such as electroshock therapy (convulsive treatment) or psychiatric surgery (Cal. Prob. Code §§ 4652(b),(c))
- authorize sterilization or abortion (Cal. Prob. Code §§ 4652(d),(e))

- authorize, condone, or approve mercy killing (Cal. Prob. Code § 4653), or
- authorize any act that exceeds the limits you place on the agent in your advance directive (Cal. Prob. Code § 4681(a)).

3. Your Health Care Agent's Legal Responsibilities

Your agent is required by law to follow any health care instructions you include in your advance directive, as well as any other wishes for treatment that the agent knows about. (Cal. Prob. Code § 4684.)

If your agent doesn't know what you would want in a given situation, the agent must make a decision for you based on what he or she believes to be in your best interests. When considering what would be best for you, your agent is required to consider all that he or she knows about your personal values and beliefs. For this reason, it's always a good idea to discuss your feelings about health care with your agent in addition to completing your advance directive.

EXAMPLE: Terrence prepares an advance directive appointing his partner, Susan, as his agent. He gives her the authority to make all medical decisions for him and doesn't write out any specific instructions in his advance directive. Several years later, Terrence is diagnosed with an aggressive form of colon cancer. In the months after his diagnosis, he and Susan have several long talks about the kind of care Terrence wants when he is close to death, as well as how he wants his body treated after death and what kind of memorial service he wants. As Terrence's death approaches, Susan attempts to follow Terrence's desires as much as possible, eventually lobbying his doctors to stop chemotherapy and other invasive treatments so that Terrence can die peacefully at home as he wished. After his death, she draws on their conversations to arrange for his burial and plan a small memorial gathering at the park near his childhood home.

Your agent is not permitted to make any decisions about your health care to which you object. (Cal. Prob. Code § 4689.) If your agent believes that you lack the ability to make medical decisions that are in your own best interest, he or she may ask a judge to step in, either to enforce the wishes you set out in your own advance directive or, if you expressed no wishes, to allow your agent to make a decision despite your objection. (See Cal. Prob. Code §§ 4765(d), 4766(a).)

4. Choosing Your Health Care Agent

The person you name as your health care agent should be someone you trust absolutely—and someone with whom you feel confident discussing your wishes. Your agent need not agree with your wishes for your medical care, but must completely respect your right to get the kind of treatment you want.

Your agent may be your spouse or partner, relative, or close friend. Keep in mind that your agent may have to fight to assert your wishes in the face of a stubborn medical establishment—and against the wishes of family members who may be driven by their own beliefs and interests, rather than yours. If you foresee the possibility of a conflict in enforcing your wishes, be sure to choose an agent who is strong-willed and assertive.

While you need not name someone who lives in the same city or state as you do, proximity is one factor to consider. If you have a long illness, your agent may be called upon to spend weeks or even months near your bedside, making sure medical personnel abide by your wishes for your medical treatment.

If you make a durable power of attorney for Finances (see Chapter 4) to name someone to manage your finances if you become incapacitated, it's usually wise to name the same person as both your agent for health care and your agent for finances. If you feel that you must name different people, be very sure you name agents who get along well and will be able to work together. You wouldn't, for example, want your agent for finances to interfere with your health care wishes by stalling or resisting

payment of medical or insurance bills, two things over which your agent for finances will have control.

We show you how to name your agent in Section C, Part 1, below.

Don't Name a Health Care Provider as Your Agent

⚠ **California law prohibits the following people from serving as an agent under an advance directive:**

- your treating health care provider or an employee of the health care institution where you are receiving care, unless the employee is related to you (or is your registered domestic partner) or you and the employee both work for the health care institution
- an operator of a community care facility— for example, a residential rehabilitation or counseling center
- an employee of a community care facility, unless the employee is related to you (or is your registered domestic partner) or you and the employee both work at the community care facility
- an operator of a residential care facility for the elderly, or
- an employee of a residential care facility for the elderly, unless the employee is related to you (or is your registered domestic partner) or you also work at the residential care facility.

(Cal. Prob. Code § 4659.)

---

a. Naming More Than One Agent

Though you are legally permitted to name more than one person to represent you, you should name only one agent when you make your advance directive. This is true even if you know of two or more people who are suitable candidates and who agree to undertake the job together. There may be problems, brought on by passing time and human nature, with naming people to share the job. In the critical time during which they would be overseeing your wishes and directing your care, they might disagree, rendering them ineffective as lobbyists on your behalf. Feuding agents could even end up settling their dispute in court, further delaying and confusing your care.

If you fear that those close to you may feel hurt if you name someone else to represent you, take some time to talk with them to explain your choice. Or, if there are several people you'd feel comfortable naming, you might even let them decide among themselves who the agent will be. If you approve of their choice, you can accept it—and name the others as alternate agents in case your first choice can't serve.

b. Naming an Alternate Agent

California's advance directive form permits you to name one or two alternate agents to represent you if your first choice is unable to take the job for any reason or resigns after your advance directive takes effect. Alternates serve one at a time, in the order that you specify.

It's a good idea to name at least one alternate agent, but you should be as thoughtful about naming your alternates as you are about choosing your first-choice: be sure to name people who will represent you well if the need arises.

We show you how to name alternate agents in Section C, Part 1, below.

5. If You Do Not Name a Health Care Agent

If you do not know of anyone you trust to oversee your medical care, it's not necessary to name an agent. In fact, it is better not to name anyone than to name someone who is not comfortable with the directions you leave—or who is not likely to assert your wishes strongly.

But even if you don't name an agent, you should still complete the rest of the advance directive, stating any health care directions about which you feel strongly. Even without an agent, medical personnel are required to follow your written wishes for health care—or to find someone who will care for you in

the way you have directed. If you do not name a health care agent, be certain to discuss your wishes for medical care with a doctor or hospital representative likely to be involved in providing that care.

C. Preparing Your Advance Directive

This book contains the California advance health care directive form on CD-ROM and as a tear-out form in Appendix B; you can use either one. If you use the form on CD-ROM, you will use your word processor to complete your form, according to the instructions below.

If you choose the tear-out form, begin by making a few photocopies of the blank form. You can use one for a draft and save a clean one for the final document—the one you will sign and have notarized or witnessed. It's best to complete it using a typewriter (if you can find one), though filling in the blanks by hand is legally permissible. If you must handprint your document, print legibly and use black ink. Don't erase, white out, or cross out anything in your form, unless the document specifically states that you may cross out words. If you are directed to cross out something, keep it simple: just draw a straight line through the unwanted text.

This section takes you through the form one part at a time. There's a sample form at the end, so you can see what a filled-in form looks like. Keep in mind, however, that depending on your wishes, your completed form may look very different from the sample.

Part 1: Power of Attorney for Health Care

Part 1 of the advance directive is called your power of attorney for health care. This is where you:

- name the primary and alternate agents who will make health care decisions for you if you are unable to do so yourself (or if you choose not to)
- place any limits on the powers you want your agent to have under your advance directive, and
- indicate whether you want your agent's authority to take effect immediately or only after a doctor finds that you are incapacitated.

(1) Designation of Agent

Begin by filling in your own name and address in the first two blanks of the form. Then enter the complete name, address, and phone numbers of your first-choice agent on the next several lines. It's important to include correct phone numbers; health care providers should be able to make quick contact with your agent if necessary. If a number changes later, it's okay to write the new number into the form. Be sure to notify anyone who has a copy of your document that your agent's phone number has changed.

After you name your agent, you can name up to two alternate agents by entering their names and contact information in the next two sets of lines. You should appoint at least one alternate if you know someone you trust enough to take the job. (See Section B4, above.)

(2) Agent's Authority to Make Medical Decisions

After you name your agent and alternates, Section (2) of Part 1 gives you the opportunity to place limits on their authority. Any limits you set will apply to your agent and alternate agents alike. If you do not place any restrictions, your agent will have broad powers, as discussed in Section B1, above.

As you consider your agent's powers, keep in mind that in Part 2 of the advance directive, you will be asked to enter your specific health care instructions, if any, and that your agent is required to follow these instructions. You do not need to enter your instructions twice by placing corresponding restrictions on your agent here. For example, if you will state in Part 2 that you do not wish to receive life-prolonging medical treatment at the end of your life, you do not have to use this part of the form to forbid your agent to authorize such treatment.

So what kind of restrictions might you want to include here? One might be to give your agent only the authority to carry out the health care wishes you specify in your advance directive, and not to make other medical decisions for you. If that's what you want, you can add a paragraph like this one:

> My agent's authority is limited to supervising and enforcing the wishes for medical care that I have expressed in this advance directive. My agent may take all actions on my behalf that are necessary to enforce my written wishes.

But think carefully before you add limiting language to your document. One of the most important reasons for appointing a health care agent is so that he or she can respond to the needs of your situation as it develops. Your medical needs may change in ways that you cannot now foresee, and an agent who has full power can act for you no matter what the circumstances.

Giving Your Agent Power to Decide Where You Will Live

At some point, you may need to move from your own home into a home or facility where you can receive ongoing medical or personal care. As discussed in Chapter 1, Section G1, California law lets you give your health care agent the power to decide where you will live. If you don't give your agent this power and specify any wishes you have about your residence, your loved ones will have to work out this decision among themselves if the issue ever comes up.

If you want your health care agent to have the authority to decide where you will live, you can add a paragraph like one of the following to your document:

- My agent may determine where I will live.
- Though I wish to remain at home as long as possible, if my agent determines that I am no longer able to reside at home, then my agent may choose where I will live.
- My agent may determine where I will live. However, if I must move to a nursing facility, I would prefer to move to the Hilldale Home on Orange Street in San Rafael.

(3) When Agent's Authority Becomes Effective

Check the box in Section (3) of the form if you wish to make your agent's authority effective immediately. (See Section A2, above.)

(4) Agent's Obligation

You don't have to do anything in Section (4) of the form. This paragraph simply restates your agent's duties under the law: to follow your instructions and make decisions in your best interest.

(5) Agent's Authority to Make Post-Death Decisions

Unless you state otherwise in Section (5), your agent will have the power to make anatomical gifts, authorize an autopsy, and direct the disposition of your body after death. You will have the opportunity to state your specific wishes about organ donation in Part 3 of the advance directive—and your agent must follow your directions. If you want to place any additional limits on your agent's authority, enter them on the blank lines in this section. Here are a few examples:

My agent may not authorize the donation of any of my organs, tissues, or body parts after death.

After death, I do not wish to be embalmed and I prefer that my body be cremated.

I direct that my agent follow the instructions in the attached letter directing the disposition of my body and other final arrangements.

The expenses of carrying out your final arrangements—services, cremation or burial, and the like—are usually paid from funds you leave at your death. If there isn't enough money in your estate when you die, your close family members will be expected to pay after-death costs. Your health care agent is liable for these costs only if your agent specifically agrees to pay them, or if the agent makes specific decisions resulting in reasonable costs that your own funds are unable to cover. (Cal. Health & Safety Code § 7100.)

Stating Your Wishes for Final Arrangements

Anyone who has lost a loved one knows how agonizing it can be to decide what he or she would have wanted as a commemoration. And most people have attended funerals or other after-death services that seem obviously unsuited to the person who has died.

Letting your survivors know in detail what kind of body disposition and ceremonies you envision saves them the pain of making such decisions at what is likely to be a difficult time for them. And planning some of these details in advance can help save money, too. Wise comparison shopping—for mortuary services, a coffin, urn, gravesite, or other after-death needs—can keep costs reasonable.

The best way to give direction to your loved ones about your wishes for final arrangements is to write them down in a letter, providing as much detail as you can. You can give the letter to your loved ones, and attach it to your advance directive if you like.

Your letter might include:

- the name of the mortuary or other institution that will handle your burial or cremation
- whether you wish to be embalmed
- the type of casket or container in which you will be buried or cremated, including whether you want it present at any after-death ceremony
- the details of any ceremony you want before the burial or cremation, including specific clothing and jewelry in which you want your body to be attired
- whom your pallbearers will be
- how your body will be transported to the cemetery and gravesite
- where your remains will be buried, stored, or scattered
- the details of any ceremony you want to accompany the burial, interment, or scattering
- the details of any marker that will show where your remains are buried or interred
- any epitaph you wish placed on your burial marker, and
- the details of any ceremony you want held after you are buried or cremated.

Getting help with final arrangements. For more information and help making your final arrangements, you can contact the Funeral Consumers Alliance at 800-458-5563 or online at www.funerals.org. If you want help crafting such a final arrangements letter, you can use *Quicken WillMaker Plus* (Nolo). The computer program walks you step-by-step through the process of creating a final arrangements letter, and provides other valuable legal documents you may need, including a will or living trust.

(6) Nomination of Conservator

If a court ever needs to appoint a conservator (see Section A4, above) to oversee your medical decisions and arrange for your personal care (clothing, food, and shelter), Section (6) of the advance directive automatically nominates your health care agent for that position. If your agent is not willing or available to act as your conservator, your document nominates your alternate agents, in the order named. This is what most people want, because in selecting an agent and alternates they have already given much thought to choosing the best person to act.

If you do not wish to include this nomination in your form for some reason, you can delete the entire clause—using your word processor if you are completing the form with the CD-ROM, or by retyping the form if you are using the tear-out version.

Part 2: Instructions for Health Care

Because health care directives sprang from the Right to Die movement, many people tend to think of them as documents appropriate only for directing that life-prolonging procedures be withdrawn or withheld. However, an advance directive is really a way to direct doctors to give you whatever type of medical care you want, within reality and reason. For example, some people want to reinforce that they would like to receive all medical treatment that is available—and an advance directive is the proper place to specify that.

(7) End-of-Life Decisions

In Section (7), the California advance directive asks you to state your preferences about life-prolonging treatments or procedures when you are at the end of your life. Basically, the form gives you two choices: You can request that you be kept alive as long as possible, or that your life not be prolonged in certain end-of-life situations. You can supplement these choices by writing in your own instructions in Section (9) of your advance directive. (See below.)

This section briefly discusses and defines medical procedures that are most often deemed "life-prolonging." It's best if you at least read quickly through the definitions so that you understand your choices. However, if you are firmly resolved to direct that all procedures be provided—or that all procedures be withheld—you can skip these definitions and simply check the box in this section that indicates your preference:

- Check box (a) if you do not wish to receive life-prolonging treatment. This means that your life will not be prolonged if you (1) have an incurable and irreversible condition that will result in your death within a relatively short time, (2) are in a permanent coma, or (3) are seriously ill such that, in the opinion of your agent, the likely risks to you of treatment would outweigh the benefits you might receive.
- Check box (b) if you do wish to receive life-prolonging treatment. This means that doctors must prolong your life as long as possible, no matter how poor the prognosis, within the limits of generally accepted health care standards.

If you are not sure what you want, read about the treatments listed below and consider how you feel about receiving them when you are close to death. Bear in mind that the available medical procedures will change over time. Technological advances mean that currently unfathomable procedures and treatments will become available, and treatments that are now common will become obsolete. Also, the treatments that are available vary drastically by region, depending on the sophistication and funding levels of local medical facilities.

When completing your advance directive, the best that you can do is to become familiar with the kinds of medical procedures that are most commonly administered to patients who are seriously ill. The best that we can do is to provide you with clear explanations. Both of these feats will help you produce an advance directive that accurately reflects your wishes.

a. Transfusions of Blood and Blood Products

Partial or full blood transfusions may be recommended to combat diseases that impair the blood system, to foster healing after a blood loss, or to replenish blood lost through surgery, disease, or injury. "Blood products" means different components of blood: fluids (called plasma) and blood cells.

b. Cardiopulmonary Resuscitation (CPR)

Cardiopulmonary resuscitation (CPR) is used when a person's heart or breathing has stopped. CPR includes applying physical pressure and using mouth-to-mouth resuscitation. Electrical shocks are also used if available. CPR is often accompanied by intravenous drugs used to normalize body systems. A final step in CPR is often attaching the patient to a respirator to help breathing. A respirator may be temporary, though some patients—those in a coma, for example—may be kept on a respirator until the end of life.

c. Diagnostic Tests

Diagnostic tests are commonly used to evaluate urine, blood, and other body fluids and to check on all bodily functions. Diagnostic tests can include X-rays and more sophisticated tests of brainwaves or other internal body systems. Some diagnostic tests—including surgery—can be expensive and invasive, producing pain and other side effects.

d. Dialysis

A dialysis machine is used to clean and add essential substances to the blood—through tubes placed in blood vessels or into the abdomen—when kidneys do not function properly. The entire cleansing process takes three or more hours and is performed on most dialysis patients two to three times a week.

With portable dialysis machines, some dialysis patients can perform the procedure at home themselves, rather than in a hospital or other facility.

e. Administration of Drugs

The most common and most controversial drugs given to seriously ill or comatose patients are antibiotics—administered by mouth, through a feeding tube, or by injection. Antibiotics are used to arrest and squelch infectious diseases. Patients in very weakened conditions may not respond even to massive doses of antibiotics.

Many health care providers argue that infections can actually be a benefit to those in advanced stages of an illness, since they may render a patient unconscious, and presumably not in pain, or help to speed the dying process. Others contend that if an antibiotic can eliminate symptoms of an illness, it is almost always the proper medical treatment.

Drugs may also be used to eliminate or alleviate pain. When completing your advance directive, you can give specific instructions about pain medication in Section (8). (See below.)

f. Use of a Respirator

A mechanical respirator or ventilator assists or takes over breathing for a patient by pumping air in and out of the lungs. These machines dispense a regulated amount of air into the lungs at a set rate—and periodically purge the lungs. Patients are connected to respirators either by a tube that goes through the mouth and throat into the lung or attaches directly through the lung surgically.

Respirators are often used to stabilize patients who are suffering from an acute trauma or breathing crisis. Once a patient has been attached to a respirator, most doctors will resist removing the machinery because of the risk of the patient's death, unless there is clear written direction that the patient does not wish to remain on a respirator.

g. Surgery

Surgical procedures such as amputation are sometimes used to stem the spread of life-threatening infections or to keep vital organs functioning. Major surgery such as a heart bypass may also be performed on patients who are terminally ill or comatose. You might want to consider the cost, time spent recovering from the invasive surgery, and the ultimate prognosis in deciding whether to include surgery in your final medical treatment.

(8) Relief From Pain

The next section of the form deals with a controversial issue: treatment to alleviate pain, sometimes called "comfort care." Medical experts disagree on whether a patient who is comatose or close to death from a terminal illness can feel pain, so they also debate whether such patients benefit from pain control medications. There is also disagreement over whether administering drugs to make a person comfortable or alleviate pain will also have the effect of prolonging the person's life. An additional complication in some cases is that high doses of pain drugs can impair respiration—and so hasten death in a seriously ill patient.

California's advance directive form assumes that you want relief from pain and discomfort at all times, even if pain medication hastens your death. Section (8) specifically states that you want to receive treatment that alleviates pain, no matter what your other wishes for care. If you prefer, however, you may modify or change these instructions by entering your wishes on the blank lines in Section (8).

(9) Other Wishes

In Section (9) of the advance directive, you can provide any additional instructions for your health care. You don't need to use this section if you feel that the previous provisions accurately and completely state your wishes, but if you have more to say, this is the place to do it.

Individual health care instructions are virtually unlimited in their scope and the way they can be written. Here, we discuss just some of the additions and modifications that you may wish to make. If there are specific issues that concern you and aren't covered here, talk to your doctor.

a. Specific Instructions

You may have strong feelings about what medical care you want to receive, for any number of reasons. You may have watched someone close to you either suffer terribly or miraculously improve as the result of a particular kind of care, such as prolonged attachment to a respirator or the administration of antibiotics. You may have moral objections to either receiving or withholding certain types of treatments. Or perhaps you are quite up-to-date on medical technology and the advantages and disadvantages of various procedures and medications and wish to dictate your care based on your understanding of what's medically most appropriate. Here are a few examples of the types of statements you can add to your form:

> Although I have indicated that I do not wish to receive life-prolonging treatment, if I have any of the conditions listed in Section (7) of this advance directive, I do want to receive any drug therapies that my primary physician recommends.

> Although I have indicated that I wish to receive life-prolonging treatment, if I have any of the conditions listed in Section (7) of this advance directive, I do not wish to receive CPR or to remain on a respirator for longer than one week.

> Although I have indicated that I wish to receive life-prolonging treatment, if I have any of the conditions listed in Section (7) of this advance directive, I do not wish to receive surgical treatment.

b. Artificially Administered Food and Water

If you cannot communicate to others your preferences for your own health care, it is also likely that you will not be able to voluntarily take in water or food through your mouth. The medical solution to this is to provide you with food and water—as a mix of nutrients and fluids—through tubes inserted in a vein,. into your stomach through your nose, or directly into your stomach through a surgical incision, depending on your condition.

Intravenous (IV) feeding, where fluids are introduced through a vein in an arm or a leg, is a short-term procedure. Tube feeding through the nose, through the stomach, intestines, or largest vein (the vena cava) can be carried on indefinitely.

Controversies over artificially administered food and water still simmer because medical experts disagree about whether its purpose is to sustain life or to cure an illness. In California, you will receive artificial nutrition and hydration unless your agent directs otherwise or you provide specific instructions about it. To make clear your wishes, you may want to include in your advance directive a statement like one of the following:

> Regardless of my condition, it is my desire to receive nutrition and hydration in all ways possible.

> If I have any of the conditions listed in Section (7) of this advance directive, I do not wish to receive nutrition and hydration by any artificial means.

> If I have any of the conditions listed in Section (7) of this advance directive, I do not wish to receive nutrition and hydration by any artificial means unless it is necessary for my comfort or to alleviate pain.

> I do not want artificial nutrition and hydration under any circumstances except for the treatment of a temporary condition in which I am unable to eat or drink and then only for a short time. If, within a short period (as determined by my agent after consulting my physician), there is no benefit to me, then I instruct that artificial nutrition and hydration be withdrawn.

c. Directing Health Care for Different Situations

If you don't feel comfortable checking the box rejecting life-prolonging treatment in the circumstances listed, you may prefer to specify the kinds of care you want to receive in different situations. For example, someone facing the diagnosis of a terminal illness may feel that the best medical care under such circumstances would be to have as much pain and suffering alleviated as possible through drugs and IVs, without any heroic medical maneuvers, such as invasive surgery or additional painful diagnostic tests.

But the same person considering treatment for a permanent coma may choose to hold out hope for the possibility of some medical cure for the condition —and direct that all possible medical treatments be administered if they become comatose. Or that person may feel strongly that life in a coma would completely lack meaning—and direct that all medical procedures, including food, water, and pain medication, be discontinued.

Here are some samples on which you might model your directions:

> If I am diagnosed with an incurable injury, disease, or illness and if the application of life-sustaining procedures would serve only to artificially prolong the moment of my death, then I desire that all life-prolonging treatment be withheld or removed. However, I wish to continue to receive pain medication, nutrition, and hydration until my death.

> If I have been in a coma for at least one week and two qualified physicians familiar with my condition have diagnosed the coma as irreversible, then I desire that all life-sustaining treatment—including nutrition, hydration, and pain medication—be removed or withheld.

> If I am diagnosed to be in a permanent coma, I want my life to be prolonged for as long as possible.

> If in my agent's judgment the risks and burdens to me of the proposed treatment outweigh the expected benefits, then I desire that all life-prolonging treatment be withheld or withdrawn. I desire that my agent consider relief from suffering, preservation or restoration of functioning, and the quality as well as the extent of my life when making decisions concerning life-prolonging treatment.

> If I develop Alzheimer's disease, I would like all noninvasive life-prolonging treatments such as artificial nutrition, fluids, and antibiotics as long as I have the ability to meaningfully interact with my family and friends, but I do not want highly intrusive treatments such as CPR, a respirator, or kidney dialysis. However, if I lose the capacity for meaningful interaction, I want only treatments that will make me more comfortable and free from pain. I would then not want artificial hydration or nutrition or antibiotics.

I do not wish to receive life-prolonging treatment if I am unable to live at home.

I do not wish to have life-saving surgery performed if two licensed physicians familiar with my condition determine that I will never able to walk or talk again.

If You Might Become Pregnant

If there is a chance you might be pregnant when your advance directive takes effect, this is the place to state whether or not you want your health care wishes to be carried out as written. Here are some clauses to help you write out your wishes:

If I am pregnant, I direct that my wishes for health care be given no effect during the course of my pregnancy.

If I am pregnant, I direct that my wishes for health care be given no effect if my primary physician believes that the fetus can develop to the point of live birth. Otherwise, I direct that my wishes for health care be carried out as written.

If I am pregnant, I direct that my wishes for health care be carried out as written.

For a discussion of the possible effects of pregnancy on your advance directive, see Section A3, above.

Part 3: Donation of Organs at Death

Part 3 of the advance directive allows you to state whether you want to donate any of your organs, tissues, or body parts after you die. This decision is, of course, a very personal matter. Here's some information that may help you decide whether or not you want to be a donor.

a. The Need for Donated Organs

Many Californians are in dire need of organ transplants. More than 15,000 people in this state (and more than 80,000 nationwide) are currently waiting for life-saving organ transplant surgery—and based on current rates of donation, one in three of them will die before receiving a transplant. Although the number of organ donations in California has been slowly and steadily on the rise, the need for organs still far exceeds the number of organs donated.

Ethnicity and Organ Donation

Because patients are less likely to reject transplanted tissue or organs donated by someone who is genetically similar, there is a need for organs from persons of all ethnic backgrounds.

But there is a special need for donations from people who are members of racial and ethnic minorities in the United States, because certain diseases of the kidney, heart, lung, pancreas, and liver occur more frequently in these minority populations than in the general population. For example, African-Americans, Asian and Pacific Islanders, and Hispanics are three times more likely to suffer from end-stage kidney disease than whites. Native Americans are four times more likely than whites to suffer from diabetes. Sometimes, organ transplant is the best—or the only—way to treat these diseases.

b. Religious Views and Concerns

Most major religions support organ donation. Reverence for life is the basis for almost all religious traditions, and organ donation is viewed as a life-saving act of compassion and generosity. Donated organs must be removed immediately after death, however, and some religions strongly believe that a deceased person's body should remain undisturbed, at least for a number of days, to benefit the consciousness of the deceased person as it separates from the body. For the practitioner of a religion that holds both of these views—such as many types of Buddhism—a dilemma may arise. On one hand, it is beneficial and an act of compassion to donate organs, while on the other, it does not allow the body to remain undisturbed. If you are uncertain about the right choice for you, it may be helpful to discuss the issue with your religious or spiritual adviser.

For a brief statement of different religions' views on organ donation, you can visit www.transweb.org.

c. Costs of Organ Donation

It will not cost your family anything if you want to donate your organs. The recipient pays the expenses, usually through insurance, Medicare, or Medicaid.

d. The Organ Donation Procedure

Before an organ is removed from a donor, two doctors who are not involved in the transplantation must declare that the patient is "irretrievably deceased" and brain-dead. Then the body is kept on a respirator to keep blood flowing though the organ until it can be removed and given to a waiting recipient. All of this usually takes about 24 hours.

Donation does not disfigure the body and does not interfere with having a funeral, even an open-casket service.

e. Specifying Your Wishes

Your advance directive is a good place to state your wishes regarding organ donation. Here's how to complete Part 3 of the form:

- Check box (a) if you want to donate any needed organs, tissues, or body parts.

- Check box (b) to specify the organs, tissues, or body parts that you are willing to donate. If you check this box, you must list the specific body parts—such as your corneas, heart, liver, kidneys, skin, or lungs—on the lines that follow the box.

Part (c) allows you to limit the purposes of your gift. If you don't want to place any restrictions on your gift, leave Part (c) as it is. But if you don't want your gift to be used for one or more of the listed purposes—transplant, therapy, research, or education—cross out any purposes you don't want.

If you do not wish to donate any organs, tissues, or body parts, you can leave this part of the form blank. You may also want to restrict your agent's power to authorize donation of your body parts, as shown in Part 1, Section (5), above.

 Customizing your form. If you are making your advance directive using the CD-ROM and you don't want to donate organs or other body parts after your death, you can delete Part 3 of the form. But if you do so, be careful. Make sure to renumber the remaining parts and paragraph numbers so that everything stays in order.

If you use your advance directive to state that you wish to donate organs, there are a couple of other steps you may also want to take to be sure your wishes are carried out. First, you may want to obtain a donor card from the local Department of Motor Vehicles. You simply fill out the card and keep it with your driver's license; there's also a small sticker that you can attach to the front of your license to show that you are a donor. This can alert others to your wishes in the event of an accident, when your advance directive may not be immediately available.

Second, and most important, you should discuss your views about organ donation with your health care agent, close relatives, and friends. Even if you've put your wishes in your advance directive and completed a donor card from the DMV, it's possible that an objection by a close relative could defeat your wishes after your death. The best thing you can do is let those close to you know that you feel strongly about donating your organs.

The California Organ and Tissue Donor Registry

To encourage people to become organ donors, and to facilitate matches between organ donors and recipients, California is in the process of creating a state organ and tissue registry. All Californians who want to be organ donors will be able to list themselves in the state's central database. When the registry is available, you will be able to obtain forms and information through the California Department of Motor Vehicles.

More information. To learn more about organ donation, see the Health and Human Services Department's website at www.organdonor.gov or call 800-55-DONOR (800-553-6667).

Part 4: Primary Physician

Here, if you like, you can enter the name of and contact information for your primary physician (and an alternate primary physician) who will oversee your medical care if possible. You will probably want to do this if you already have an established relationship with a doctor you trust and with whom you have discussed—or will discuss—your health care wishes. (For information about the importance of discussing your wishes with those who are likely to be involved with your care, see Section D2, below.)

If you have more than one doctor and you're not sure which one to pick, think about who would do the best job of supervising your overall care. This may be your family doctor or general practitioner, rather than a specialist. If you're having trouble deciding, you may want to have conversations with each of them. After talking about your wishes, you may find that one of them seems more comfortable taking on the responsibility of managing your care, or that you have a better sense of whom you should pick. Remember you can name one as your first choice and another as an alternate.

If you don't have an established relationship with a doctor—and many people don't nowadays—you'll do just as well to leave this part of your form blank and let your agent choose your health care providers if and when that becomes necessary.

Customizing your form. If you are using the CD-ROM to prepare your document and you don't want to name a primary physician, you can delete Part 4 from the form. Make sure you renumber the remaining parts and paragraphs accordingly.

Part 5: Making Your Advance Directive Legal

In this last part of your advance directive, you will finalize your document by signing it in front of either a notary public or two witnesses. (You don't have to do both.) If you are a resident in a nursing home, you must also comply with a special witnessing requirement. This section explains each alternative.

a. Notarization

A notary public is someone who is certified to verify signatures on documents. You can locate a notary by looking in the Yellow Pages of the telephone book; most banks, insurance offices, and title companies also have a notary on staff. Most charge a small fee—about $10—for notarizing documents.

If you go to a notary, bring along some identification, such as your driver's license, that will help prove that you are who you say you are. The notary will watch you sign your advance directive (in Paragraph (13) of the document) and then sign it and stamp it with an official seal.

b. Witnesses

If you don't want to have your document notarized, you can sign it in front of two witnesses instead. Your witnesses must watch you sign your document and then sign the witness statements in Section (14).

Sample Advance Health Care Directive

Advance Health Care Directive

Explanation

You have the right to give instructions about your own health care. You also have the right to name someone else to make health care decisions for you. This form lets you do either or both of these things. It also lets you express your wishes regarding donation of organs and the designation of your primary physician. If you use this form, you may complete or modify all or any part of it. You are free to use a different form.

Part 1 of this form is a power of attorney for health care. Part 1 lets you name another individual as agent to make health care decisions for you if you become incapable of making your own decisions or if you want someone else to make those decisions for you now even though you are still capable. You may also name an alternate agent to act for you if your first choice is not willing, able, or reasonably available to make decisions for you. (Your agent may not be an operator or employee of a community care facility or a residential care facility where you are receiving care, or your supervising health care provider or employee of the health care institution where you are receiving care, unless your agent is related to you, is your registered domestic partner, or is a coworker.)

Unless the form you sign limits the authority of your agent, your agent may make all health care decisions for you. This form has a place for you to limit the authority of your agent. You need not limit the authority of your agent if you wish to rely on your agent for all health care decisions that may have to be made. If you choose not to limit the authority of your agent, your agent will have the right to:

- Consent or refuse consent to any care, treatment, service, or procedure to maintain, diagnose, or otherwise affect a physical or mental condition.
- Select or discharge health care providers and institutions.

- Approve or disapprove diagnostic tests, surgical procedures, and programs of medication.
- Direct the provision, withholding, or withdrawal of artificial nutrition and hydration and all other forms of health care, including cardiopulmonary resuscitation.
- Make anatomical gifts, authorize an autopsy, and direct disposition of remains.

Part 2 of this form lets you give specific instructions about any aspect of your health care, whether or not you appoint an agent. Choices are provided for you to express your wishes regarding the provision, withholding, or withdrawal of treatment to keep you alive, as well as the provision of pain relief. Space is also provided for you to add to the choices you have made or for you to write out any additional wishes. If you are satisfied to allow your agent to determine what is best for you in making end-of-life decisions, you need not fill out Part 2 of this form.

Part 3 of this form lets you express an intention to donate your bodily organs and tissues following your death. Part 4 of this form lets you designate a physician to have primary responsibility for your health care.

After completing this form, sign and date the form at the end. The form must be signed by two qualified witnesses or acknowledged before a notary public. Give a copy of the signed and completed form to your physician, to any other health care providers you may have, to any health care institution at which you are receiving care, and to any health care agents you have named. You should talk to the person you have named as agent to make sure that he or she understands your wishes and is willing to take the responsibility. You have the right to revoke this advance health care directive or replace this form at any time.

Sample Advance Health Care Directive (continued)

Part 1: Power of Attorney for Health Care

(1)   Designation of Agent: I _____Chester Larkin_____ , of

_16 Deerwood Drive, San Francisco_____,

California, designate the following individual as my agent to make health care decisions for me:

_Arthur Stimple_____
Name of Individual You Choose as Agent

_16 Deerwood Drive_____
Address

San Francisco	_CA_	_94114_
City	State	Zip Code
_(415) 444-5555_	_(415) 444-1234_	
Home Phone	Work Phone	

First Alternate Agent (Optional): If I revoke my agent's authority or if my agent is not willing, able, or reasonably available to make a health care decision for me, I designate as my first alternate agent:

_Karen Larkin_____
Name of Individual You Choose as First Alternate Agent

_3421 Euclid Avenue_____
Address

Berkeley	_CA_	_94709_
City	State	Zip Code
_(510) 548-5588_	_(510) 894-4000_	
Home Phone	Work Phone	

Second Alternate Agent (Optional): If I revoke the authority of my agent and first alternate agent or if neither is willing, able, or reasonably available to make a health care decision for me, I designate as my second alternate agent:

_____
Name of Individual You Choose as Second Alternate Agent

_____
Address

City	State	Zip Code
Home Phone	Work Phone	

(2)   Agent's Authority: My agent is authorized to make all health care decisions for me, including decisions to provide, withhold, or withdraw artificial nutrition and hydration and all other forms of health care to keep me alive, except as I state here:

_____

_____

_____

_____

_____

Add Additional Sheets If Needed

Sample Advance Health Care Directive (continued)

(3) **When Agent's Authority Becomes Effective:** My agent's authority becomes effective when my primary physician determines that I am unable to make my own health care decisions unless I mark the following box. If I mark this box ☐, my agent's authority to make health care decisions for me takes effect immediately.

(4) **Agent's Obligation:** My agent shall make health care decisions for me in accordance with this power of attorney for health care, any instructions I give in Part 2 of this form, and my other wishes to the extent known to my agent. To the extent my wishes are unknown, my agent shall make health care decisions for me in accordance with what my agent determines to be in my best interest. In determining my best interest, my agent shall consider my personal values to the extent known to my agent.

(5) **Agent's Postdeath Authority:** My agent is authorized to make anatomical gifts, authorize an autopsy, and direct disposition of my remains, except as I state here or in Part 3 of this form:

I want my body to be cremated and my ashes to be scattered off the Marin Headlands.

Add Additional Sheets If Needed

(6) **Nomination of Conservator:** If a conservator of my person needs to be appointed for me by a court, I nominate the agent designated in this form. If that agent is not willing, able, or reasonably available to act as conservator, I nominate the alternate agents whom I have named, in the order designated.

Part 2: Instructions for Health Care

If you fill out this part of the form, you may strike any wording you do not want.

(7) **End-of-Life Decisions:** I direct that my health care providers and others involved in my care provide, withhold, or withdraw treatment in accordance with the choice I have marked below:

    ☒ (a) Choice Not to Prolong Life
        I do not want my life to be prolonged if (1) I have an incurable and irreversible condition that will result in my death within a relatively short time, (2) I become unconscious and, to a reasonable degree of medical certainty, I will not regain consciousness, or (3) the likely risks and burdens of treatment would outweigh the expected benefits.

Sample Advance Health Care Directive (continued)

~~☐ (b) Choice to Prolong Life~~
~~I want my life to be prolonged as long as possible within the limits of generally accepted health care standards.~~

(8) **Relief From Pain:** Except as I state in the following space, I direct that treatment for alleviation of pain or discomfort be provided at all times, even if it hastens my death:

_____

_____

_____

_____

_____

Add Additional Sheets If Needed

(9) **Other Wishes:** (If you do not agree with any of the optional choices above and wish to write your own, or if you wish to add to the instructions you have given above, you may do so here.) I direct that:

I do not wish to receive artificial nutrition and hydration under any circumstances except for the treatment of a temporary condition in which I am unable to eat or drink, and then only for a short time. If, within a short time (as determined by my agent after consulting my doctor) there is no benefit to me, then I instruct that artifical nutrition and hydration be withdrawn.

_____

Add Additional Sheets If Needed

Part 3: Donation of Organs at Death

(10) Wishes for Organ Donation: Upon my death (mark applicable box):

☒ (a) I give any needed organs, tissues, or parts.

☐ (b) I give the following organs, tissues, or parts only:

_____

_____

_____

_____

_____

Add Additional Sheets If Needed

Sample Advance Health Care Directive (continued)

☐ (c) My gift is for the following purposes (strike any of the following you do not want):

(1) Transplant

(2) Therapy

(3) Research

(4) Education

Part 4: Primary Physician

(11) Designation of Primary Physician: I designate the following physician as my primary physician:

Dr. Marcia Silverstein
Name of Physician

555 9th Avenue
Address

San Francisco   CA   94118
City   State   Zip Code

(415) 261-2601
Phone

Secondary Designation: If the physician I have designated above is not willing, able, or reasonably available to act as my primary physician, I designate the following physician as my primary physician:

Name of Physician

Address

City   State   Zip Code

Phone

Part 5: Signatures

(12) Effect of Copy: A copy of this form has the same effect as the original.

(13) Signature: Sign and date the form here:

Dated: _____December 3, 2003_____

Chester Larkin
Sign Your Name

Chester Larkin
Print Your Name

Sample Advance Health Care Directive (continued)

Alternative #1: Witnesses

(14) Statement of Witnesses: I declare under penalty of perjury under the laws of California (1) that the individual who signed or acknowledged this advance health care directive is personally known to me, or that the individual's identity was proven to me by convincing evidence, (2) that the individual signed or acknowledged this advance directive in my presence, (3) that the individual appears to be of sound mind and under no duress, fraud, or undue influence, (4) that I am not a person appointed as agent by this advance directive, and (5) that I am not the individual's health care provider, an employee of the individual's health care provider, the operator of a community care facility, an employee of an operator of a community care facility, the operator of a residential care facility for the elderly, nor an employee of an operator of a residential care facility for the elderly.

First Witness

Chloe Abrams
Signature of Witness

Chloe Abrams
Print Name

2970 16th Street, San Francisco, CA 94103
Address

December 3, 2003
Date

Second Witness

James Lee
Signature of Witness

James Lee
Print Name

849 Valencia Street, San Francisco, CA 94110
Address

December 3, 2003
Date

(15) Additional Statement of Witnesses: One of the above witnesses must also sign the following declaration:

I further declare under penalty of perjury under the laws of California that I am not related to the individual executing this advance health care directive by blood, marriage, or adoption, and to the best of my knowledge, I am not entitled to any part of the individual's estate upon his or her death under a will now existing or by operation of law.

James Lee
Signature of Witness

Sample Advance Health Care Directive (continued)

Alternative #2: Notarization

Certificate of Acknowledgment of Notary Public

State of _____

County of _____ } ss

On _____, _____, before me, _____,

personally appeared _____,

personally known to me (or proved on the basis of satisfactory evidence) to be the person whose name is

subscribed to the within instrument, and acknowledged to me that he or she executed the same in his or her

authorized capacity and that by his or her signature on the instrument, the person, or the entity upon behalf

of which the person acted, executed the instrument.

WITNESS my hand and official seal.

_____

Notary Public for the State of California

[NOTARY SEAL]   My commission expires _____

(16) **SPECIAL WITNESS REQUIREMENT:** The following statement is required only if you are a patient in
a skilled nursing facility—a health care facility that provides skilled nursing care and supportive
care to patients whose primary need is for availability of skilled nursing care on an extended
basis. The patient advocate or ombudsman must sign the following statement:

Statement of Patient Advocate or Ombudsman

I declare under penalty of perjury under the laws of California that I am a patient advocate or
ombudsman as designated by the State Department of Aging and that I am serving as a witness as
required by Section 4675 of the Probate Code.

_____
Signature of Patient Advocate or Ombudsman

_____
Print Name

_____
Address

_____
Date

Your witnesses must be adults, preferably ones who live nearby and will be readily available if it's ever necessary to prove that your advance directive is valid. In addition, neither witness can be:

- your health care agent
- your health care provider, or an employee of your health care provider
- the operator or employee of a community care facility, such as a residential rehabilitation or counseling center, or
- the operator or employee of a residential care facility for the elderly.

Also, one of your witnesses must sign the witness statement in Section (15) declaring that the witness is not:

- related to you by blood, marriage, or adoption, or
- entitled to receive any part of your estate either under your will or by operation of law if you die without a will (usually, this means your close relatives).

It's not usually difficult to satisfy this last requirement. You can ask a neighbor or friend to witness your document, so long as you're not leaving that person anything in your will.

c. Patients in Skilled Nursing Facilities

If, at the time you sign your document, you are a patient in a nursing home or other health care facility that provides long-term nursing and supportive care, you must obtain the signature of the facility's patient advocate or ombudsman in Paragraph (16) of your form. This requirement applies whether you have your document notarized or witnessed, as described just above.

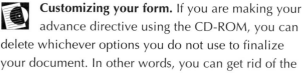 **Customizing your form.** If you are making your advance directive using the CD-ROM, you can delete whichever options you do not use to finalize your document. In other words, you can get rid of the unused notary or witness statements. Remember to renumber any paragraphs remaining at the end of your form, if necessary.

D. What to Do After You Complete Your Advance Directive

By taking the time and making the effort to draw up your advance directive, you have already done much to ensure that your wishes will be followed. The next step is to make your wishes for your future health care widely known.

1. Distributing Copies

Some people are hesitant to discuss the particulars of their medical care with other people, feeling that it is an intensely private issue. However, in the case of health care documents, you must weigh your desire for privacy against the need for the documents to be effective. Your carefully reasoned medical directive will be wasted unless you make sure it gets into the hands of the people who need to know about it.

At a minimum, give copies of your signed and completed advance directive to the doctors or medical facility most likely to be treating you and to your health care agent. Also think about giving copies to immediate family members and friends. Here's a complete list of people and institutions to whom you may want to give copies:

- any physician you consult regularly
- the agent you named in your directive
- the office of the hospital or other care facility in which you are likely to receive treatment
- the patient representative of your HMO or insurance plan (you can call your plan's business office to find out who this person is and how to make contact)
- close relatives, particularly immediate family members—spouse, children, siblings, and
- trusted friends.

A copy of your advance directive is every bit as legally valid as the original. (Your form clearly states this in Section (12).)

Registering Your Advance Directive

To increase the chances that health care providers will know you've completed an advance directive, you may want to register the document with one or both of the following services. Registering your advance directive, however, is not a substitute for directly sharing your wishes with doctors, family, and friends.

The U.S. Living Will Registry. You can put your advance directive on file free of charge by signing up through one of the health care providers or organizations listed on the registry website. After you file your advance directive, health care providers can call the registry to obtain a copy of it. The registry will release your document only to health care providers, so your personal information is kept private, like a medical record. You will receive labels to attach to your health insurance card and driver's license to alert medical personnel to the existence of your health care document. For more information, visit www.uslivingwillregistry.com or call 1-800-LIV-WILL (1-800-548-9455).

The California Secretary of State. You can register basic information about your advance directive in a database maintained by the California Secretary of State's "Special Filings Unit." The form you file states that you've made an advance directive and says where you keep the document, so that others can find it. You don't disclose the details of your health care wishes when you register. Registry information is available on request to health care providers and anyone else that you name in your registration form. Currently, doctors and hospitals rarely use the registry system to find out whether a patient has an advance directive, but it doesn't cost anything to register and it certainly can't hurt you. If health care providers begin to use the registry more frequently, it may turn out to be helpful.

The form you need to register your advance directive is available through the Secretary of State's website at www.ss.ca.gov/business/sf/forms/sf-461.pdf. Or, you can call the Special Filings Unit for more information: 916-653-3984.

2. Talking With Doctors

There is no substitute for discussing your medical preferences with the doctors who will be likely to provide your care. Unfortunately, in practice this task may be difficult. Few people have the luxury of cultivating a meaningful relationship with any individual doctor. Many of us now depend for medical care on monolithic medical centers, in which seeing the same health care provider more than once seems almost accidental.

However, if you do have a regular doctor, or if you are approaching major surgery or some other drastic medical event and have been assigned to a specialist, talk over your medical directives with him or her. If you have other concerns about your medical condition, such as the effects of certain treatments or the probability of carrying on certain life activities, discuss those, too.

3. Talking With Family Members and Friends

It is also wise to discuss your health care directives and other medical care concerns with the people who are likely to oversee or witness your care. Unfortunately, this too is sometimes frustrated by reality. Families these days are often flung far across the map. And even those who remain geographically close often stray from the Ozzie-and-Harriet ideal of family harmony.

Still, those who make the effort to discuss these issues usually find the effort worth the price. Not only do those involved get peace of mind in knowing true wishes, the knowledge can often be a bridge to closer relationships. If the topic seems too difficult to broach, consider using a relevant book, magazine article, television show, or film as a catalyst for discussion.

4. Preparing a Wallet Card

If you are involved in a serious accident or other medical emergency, a wallet card like the one below can alert emergency medical personnel to the existence of your advance directive. You may want to complete one of these cards to carry with you— keep it in a conspicuous place in your wallet—and give another card to your spouse, agent, or other person who is likely to be contacted in an emergency. Remember to make new cards if any of the information on the card changes.

You can find a tear-out wallet card in Appendix B.

Attention: Emergency Medical Personnel

I _____

[insert your name] of _____

_____ *[insert your address]*
have prepared an advance health care directive stating the type of medical care I wish to receive if I am incapacitated and unable to speak for myself. I have also appointed a health care agent to oversee my wishes. In the event of a medical emergency, please contact one of the people listed on the reverse of this card, in the order listed.

©Nolo 2003   [OVER]

My Agent: _____

_____ *[insert agent's name and phone numbers where agent can be reached in an emergency]*
My Alternate Agent: _____

_____

My Primary Physician: _____

_____

[insert your doctor's name and phone number]
My advance health care directive is located: _____

_____

[insert the location of an easy-to-find copy of your directive]

---

5. Keeping Your Documents Up to Date

It's a good idea to review your health care documents occasionally—at least once a year—to make sure they still accurately reflect your wishes. Advances in technology and changes in your health are two shifts in course that may prompt you to change your mind about the kind of health care you want.

In addition, you should consider making new documents if:

You move to another state. Most states have laws honoring advance directives that are properly prepared under the laws of another state. Nevertheless, if you move, it's a good idea to prepare a new advance directive using your new state's official form. Health care providers in your new state will be most familiar with that state's form, and this will most likely make it easier for your agent to manage your care.

You made and finalized a health care directive many years ago. California's laws governing advance directives have changed more than once in the past decade. Though your advance directive is valid if made under an old law, it's wise to keep your document up to date. Health care providers and hospitals will be most comfortable honoring the state's most recent advance directive form.

The agent you named to supervise your wishes becomes unable to do so. If your first choice as agent becomes unavailable before your document has taken effect, you may want to make a new directive to name a new agent. It's true that if you appoint an alternate agent, that person will take the job if it's ever necessary. But if you already know your agent is unavailable, it's smart to name someone new— perhaps just moving your alternate into the first position and naming another alternate to back up that person. This helps to ensure someone will always be available to make decisions for you.

If you make new advance directive, you should formally revoke your old one. (See below.)

You get divorced. If you named your spouse or registered domestic partner as your health care agent, it's wise to make a new directive to name a new agent. (See Section A4, above.)

Revocation of Advance Health Care Directive

I, ___Faith Douglass_____ ,

of the City of _____Bakersfield_____ , County of _____Kern_____ ,

State of California, revoke the advance health care directive dated ___July 12, 2000_____ ,

empowering_____Tyler Douglass_____

to make health care decisions for me. I revoke and withdraw all power and authority granted

under that directive.

Dated: ___May 3, 2002_____

_Faith Douglass_____
(Signature of Principal)

___Faith Douglass_____
(Print Principal's Name)

E. Revoking an Advance Directive

You can revoke your advance directive at any time, as long as you are of sound mind. California law presumes that you have the capacity to revoke your documents whenever you wish, so anyone who challenges your ability to revoke a document bears the burden of proving that you are no longer of sound mind. (Cal. Prob. Code § 4657.)

If you want to cancel your advance directive for any reason, it's best to do so in writing. Giving a written Notice of Revocation to your health care agent and anyone else who has a copy of your advance directive eliminates confusion and helps to ensure that your most recent wishes will be honored. We provide a simple revocation form that you can use, both on the CD-ROM and as a tear-out form in Appendix B. A sample is shown above.

How to Revoke an Advance Health Care Directive

☐ Prepare and sign a Notice of Revocation. (Unlike the advance directive itself, your signature doesn't need to be notarized or witnessed.)

☐ Deliver a copy of the Notice of Revocation to your health care agent and anyone else who has a copy of your advance directive.

☐ Destroy your original, signed advance directive.

☐ Obtain all copies of your advance directive and destroy them, too.

In addition to preparing the Notice of Revocation, you should tear up the original document and all copies. Make sure that all people who have copies of your advance directive return them to you to be destroyed.

If you have a change of heart about your health care wishes but are unable to prepare a Notice of Revocation, you can tell any health care provider—for example, a doctor or nurse when you're in the hospital—that you want to cancel your advance directive. The health care provider is required to promptly communicate your wishes to your supervising health care provider (your primary doctor) and to any health care institution where you are receiving care. (Cal. Prob. Code § 4696.) The supervising health care provider must then act quickly to note the revocation in your medical record. (Cal. Prob. Code § 4731(a).)

If, however, you wish to revoke the authority of your health care agent—not just change your health care wishes—and you are unable to do so in writing, you must communicate this directly to the doctor who is supervising your care at the time you want to revoke your document. (Cal. Prob. Code § 4695(a).) ■

Do Not Resuscitate (DNR) Orders

In addition to preparing an advance directive, you may want to complete a Prehospital Do Not Resuscitate order, or DNR order. A DNR order directs emergency medical personnel not to administer cardiopulmonary resuscitation (CPR) in the event of a medical emergency. It's called a "prehospital" DNR order because it covers emergencies that occur when you are not in the hospital—for example, if you collapse when at home. If you are hospitalized, doctors can add a DNR order to your medical record if you wish.

You may want to consider a DNR order if you:

- have a terminal illness
- have a high risk for cardiac or respiratory arrest, or
- have strong feelings against the use of CPR under any circumstances.

A. How DNR Orders Work

Emergency response teams must act quickly in a medical crisis. They do not have the time to determine whether you have a valid advance directive explaining treatments you want provided or withheld, and even if you carry a wallet card alerting emergency medical personnel to the existence of your advance directive (see Chapter 2, Section D4), they probably won't be able to obtain the document right away. If they do not know your wishes, they must provide you with all possible life-saving measures. You can make sure that emergency care providers know about your DNR order by wearing an easily identifiable bracelet, anklet, or necklace. (Instructions for ordering one are below.) If emergency personnel know of the DNR order, they will not administer CPR.

If you ask to have CPR withheld, you will not be provided with:

- chest compression
- electric shock treatments to the chest
- tubes placed in the airway to assist breathing
- artificial ventilation, or
- cardiac drugs.

B. Preparing a DNR Order

This book contains a legally valid DNR form that you can use to reject CPR in the event of a medical emergency. You can find the form on the CD-ROM or in Appendix B. A sample is shown below.

In order to make your DNR order binding on medical personnel, however, you must obtain a doctor's signature. (Cal. Prob. Code § 4780.) And a doctor may feel more comfortable signing a form that is issued by the doctor's office, or by a hospital. Use the form that you doctor prefers.

A DNR form is easy to prepare. To complete the form in this book, just fill in your name on the first blank line. Sign the form at the bottom (you're called the principal), writing in the date and your address. Then have your doctor do the same.

C. What to Do After You Complete a DNR Order

After you complete your DNR order, you can obtain a bracelet or medallion by calling the MedicAlert Foundation at 888-633-4298. They will send you an application to fill out and submit along with a copy of your signed DNR form. (You can also apply on the MedicAlert website at www.medicalert.org.) Wearing a DNR necklace or bracelet is the best way to tell emergency medical personnel that you do not wish to be resuscitated.

DNR medallions cost between $35 and $75 (more if you want to order from the "designer line"), and it will take MedicAlert about two to three weeks to process your order.

If you prepare a DNR order, discuss your decision with your family or other caretakers. Tell them where your form is located and who you want them to alert if you require emergency treatment. For example, in addition to calling 911, you may want someone to alert your primary physician that you're in trouble. Even if you are wearing identification, such as a bracelet or necklace, keep the form in an obvious place. You might consider keeping it by your bedside, on the front of your refrigerator, in your wallet, or in your suitcase if you are traveling. If your DNR

Prehospital Do Not Resuscitate (DNR) Order

I, _____Hector Viera_____ ,
direct that if my heart stops beating or if I stop breathing, no medical procedures be initiated to
resuscitate me, including chest compressions, assisted ventilations, intubation, defibrillation, or
cardiotonic medications.

I hereby agree to and request this Do Not Resuscitate (DNR) order.

If the principal's health care agent or other medical surrogate is signing this form on behalf of the
principal, by signing this form, the surrogate acknowledges that this request to forgo resuscitative
measures is consistent with the known desires of, and with the best interest of, the individual who is
the subject of the form.

Dated: _February 9, 2004_____

_Hector Viera_____
Signature of Principal

_Hector Viera_____
Print Principal's Name

_24 Ritter Road_____
Principal's Address and Phone Number

_Calexico, CA 92231_____

_(760) 761-9876_____

Dated: _February 9, 2004_____

_Alicia Machado_____
Signature of Physician

_Alicia Machado_____
Print Physician's Name

_370 E. Birch Street, Suite 205_____
Physician's Address and Phone Number

_Calexico, CA 92231_____

_(760) 761-0123_____

order is not apparent and immediately available, or if it has been altered in any way, CPR will most likely be performed.

You may also wish to give a copy of the DNR order to your physician, so that it can be made part of your medical record.

For more information about DNR orders. To find out more about DNR orders, call the California Medical Association at 916-444-5532.

D. Revoking a DNR Order

If you change your mind and want to revoke your DNR order, you should destroy the DNR form and any copies, and make sure everyone you've told about your DNR order knows that you have revoked it. There is no revocation form to fill out. And, obviously, you should remove any DNR medallions that you have been wearing. ■

Durable Powers of Attorney for Finances

As discussed in the introduction to this book, making a durable power of attorney ensures that someone you trust will have the legal authority to manage the many practical financial tasks that will arise if you become incapacitated—from paying bills to handling insurance, government benefits, and other matters. This chapter tells you what you need to know to understand and prepare your California durable power of attorney document.

A. How Durable Powers of Attorney for Finances Work

Before you jump into the process of making your durable power of attorney for finances, it's a good idea to know a little bit about how the document works in the real world. This section covers the following important issues:

- who can make a valid power of attorney
- how much it costs to make a power of attorney
- when a power of attorney becomes effective (either right away or only if you are incapacitated)
- how to make sure your power of attorney will be accepted by banks, government agencies, and others, and
- when a power of attorney ends.

1. Who Can Make a Durable Power of Attorney for Finances

You can create a valid power of attorney for finances if you are an adult (at least 18 years old) and of sound mind. For a more detailed discussion of the mental capacity requirement, see Chapter 1, Section D.

2. When Your Document Becomes Effective

There are two kinds of durable powers of attorney for finances: those that take effect immediately and those that never take effect unless a doctor (or two, if you wish) declares that you can no longer manage your financial affairs. Which kind you should choose depends, in part, on when you want your agent to begin handling tasks for you.

a. You Want Someone to Take Over Now

If you want someone to take over some or all of your affairs now, you should make your document effective as soon as you sign it. (In California, your document is effective when you sign unless you specify otherwise.) Then, your agent can begin helping you with your financial tasks right away—and can continue to do so if you later become incapacitated.

You don't have to be incapacitated to benefit from a durable power of attorney. If you make your document effective immediately, your agent can step in right away to help you manage your financial affairs. This may make sense in a number of different situations, including when:

- you are suffering from a short- or long-term illness and you don't have the energy to deal with day-to-day financial tasks
- you have an injury that makes it difficult to get to your financial institutions to take care of important money matters, or
- you've been occasionally forgetful and feel that it would be safer to have someone else keep an eye on your finances.

Even if you give your agent permission to start handling your finances before you become incapacitated, you don't have to turn over complete control. Explain to your agent what you want done. Your agent should follow your wishes carefully. And if you want your agent to consult you before taking action under the power of attorney, he or she is legally obligated to do so. If you ever become dissatisfied with the arrangement, you can revoke the durable power and end the agent's authority to act for you.

b. You Want Your Agent to Take Over Only If You Become Incapacitated

On the other hand, you may feel strongly that your agent should not take over unless you are incapacitated. In this case, you have two options. If you trust your agent to act only when it's absolutely necessary, you can go ahead and make an immediately effective document. Legally, your agent will then have the authority to act on your behalf—but won't do so unless he or she ever decides that you cannot handle your affairs yourself.

What Is Incapacity?

Incapacity means that you have lost some physical or mental abilities, but it is not a recognized medical condition. For purposes of your durable power of attorney for finances, incapacity essentially means that you no longer have the ability to handle your own financial transactions, either because you can no longer communicate your wishes or because you cannot understand:

- the rights, duties, and responsibilities created or affected by your financial decisions
- the probable consequences of your financial decisions, or
- the significant risks, benefits, and reasonable alternatives involved in your financial decisions.

(These guidelines are set out in Section 812 of the California Probate Code and Section 39 of the California Civil Code.)

Common physical causes of incapacity are problems generally associated with advancing age, such as heart attacks, strokes, and Alzheimer's disease. Incapacity can also be caused by serious accidents, drug or alcohol addiction, or degenerative diseases such as AIDS or mental illness. People sometimes move in and out of periods of incapacity. (For information about what happens if you regain capacity and want to revoke your power of attorney, see Section E.)

If you're uncomfortable giving your agent authority now, you can add language to your durable power of attorney to make what's known as a "springing" document. It won't take effect until a physician examines you and declares, in writing, that you can't manage your finances.

There are some real inconveniences involved in creating a springing power of attorney, and it's wise to consider them before you decide to make one. If you truly trust your agent, you may find that it makes more sense to create a document that takes effect immediately and then make clear to your agent when to take action.

(1) Making Your Document Effective Immediately

If you know, or reasonably believe, that you are likely to become incapacitated soon, it's probably a good idea to make your durable power of attorney effective right away. For example, this would be appropriate if you or someone you love has a serious degenerative disease and is rapidly losing the ability to manage business affairs. Or, if you are facing major surgery, you will probably want to sign an immediately effective document.

Even if you're 100% healthy now, if you're comfortable giving another person the authority to manage your affairs, and your agent is trustworthy (you shouldn't appoint anyone that you don't trust completely), you're probably better off making your document effective immediately. That avoids the hassles of creating a springing power of attorney, discussed in the following section. You can agree with your agent that no action will be taken under the document until, in the agent's opinion, you are unable to take care of your finances—or you otherwise direct them to take action. If you aren't confident that your agent will refrain from using the document for as long as you are able to handle your own affairs, think about naming someone else to represent you.

If you choose to make your document effective immediately, you and your agent should discuss what "incapacity" means to you. You'll want a clear understanding of when your agent should step in. That moment may be when your agent sees that you're too ill to pay your bills on time or that you have lost the mental acuity to make responsible decisions about your investments. Explore various scenarios with your agent until you reach an understanding of when and how your agent should exercise authority under the document.

(2) Making the Power of Attorney Effective Later

You may not want your agent to take over your financial affairs until a doctor states that you are no longer able to manage them on your own. If this is so, you can make a "springing" power of attorney. It has absolutely no effect unless and until at least one physician signs a sworn statement that you are incapacitated.

Some people prefer this kind of durable power of attorney because they're not in immediate danger of incapacity. The document simply acts as a kind of risk-free legal insurance—something to protect you if you ever need it.

And some people may like the idea of a springing document because requiring at least one doctor's statement removes any danger that an agent will make a judgment that someone is incapacitated—even if that person disagrees. Ideally, however, you will trust your agent so well that this will not be a serious concern.

There are some drawbacks to springing powers of attorney that you should consider.

First, for your document to spring into effect, your agent will have to obtain statements from one or two doctors (the number is up to you) certifying that you can no longer handle your financial affairs. Before they can sign such statements, they will need to examine you and perhaps order diagnostic tests. The process of getting the doctors' statements may be time consuming and complicated for your agent.

In addition, some people may be reluctant to accept a springing power of attorney, even though your agent has obtained the required doctors' statements and your document is perfectly legal. A bank, for example, might question whether you have, in fact, become incapacitated. These hassles could delay your agent and disrupt the handling of your finances.

With a springing durable power of attorney, someone must be responsible for judging whether or not you are incapacitated. Otherwise, there's no way for the document to go into effect. When you make a durable power of attorney using this book, you have a couple of options. You can:

- name (in your power of attorney document) one or two doctors to make the determination, or
- allow your agent to choose one or two doctors if the need arises.

Why Must a Doctor Make the Decision?

Because incapacity isn't a distinct medical condition, it may seem unnecessary to have a physician make the determination that you can no longer handle your finances. But it's almost always done that way, even though California law doesn't expressly require it.

A doctor's statement is familiar and reassuring to the people your agent will have to deal with. Banks and other institutions would probably be unwilling to rely on a statement by a family member or close friend that you are unable to handle your affairs.

However, as discussed above, if you don't want to involve doctors in this decision, you can let your agent decide when to start using the authority granted by the durable power of attorney.

A form for the doctor to sign is included in this book. A sample follows below; you can find a blank form on the enclosed CD-ROM or in Appendix B. After the physician has signed a statement documenting your incapacity, the agent can attach it to the original power of attorney. Then, if anyone questions the agent's authority to act for you, the agent can produce the statement.

If you name the doctor yourself, be sure the person you've chosen is willing to make the incapacity determination for you. And be certain you and the doctor are in basic agreement about what "incapacitated" means to you. If you decide to let your agent choose the doctor, you should have a conversation about incapacity with your agent. He or she will need to discuss the issue with the doctor if the time comes.

One Doctor or Two?

If you're comfortable with the idea of naming one doctor to make this determination, there's no need to require a second physician's statement. If it worries you to leave the decision in the hands of just one person, take a moment to consider whether you're comfortable making this power of attorney document. Do you truly trust the person who will be your agent? Do you fear that family members will make trouble for your agent and try to interfere with your plans? If you are experiencing a lot of anxiety about making the document, talk with family members and the person who will be your agent to get a clearer idea of whether they support what you are doing. If you're still uncomfortable after you've tried to talk things out, you may want to consult a lawyer about your fears.

If you name a specific doctor to certify your incapacity and that doctor is not available when a physician's statement is needed, your agent can choose another doctor to make the determination.

If no one objects to the doctor's statement that you are incapacitated, your document should take effect without any trouble. But if third parties raise a fuss (not likely, but it sometimes happens), a court may have to make the final decision about your ability to take care of yourself and your property.

3. When the Power of Attorney Ends

A durable power of attorney for finances is valid until you revoke it, you die, or there is no one to serve as your agent. Very infrequently, a court invalidates a power of attorney.

a. You Revoke the Power of Attorney

As long as you are of sound mind, you can revoke a power of attorney for finances at any time, whether or not it has taken effect. All you need to do is fill out a simple revocation form, sign it in front of a notary public, and give copies to the agent and to people or institutions the agent has been dealing with. This book contains revocation forms for you to use. (Sample forms are shown in Section E; you can find blank forms on the CD-ROM and in Appendix B.) Keep these forms on hand in case you need them later.

b. A Court Invalidates Your Power of Attorney

Even after you sign a durable power of attorney for finances, if you become incapacitated there is a remote possibility that a disgruntled relative could ask a court to appoint a conservator to manage your financial affairs.

It's rare, but a power of attorney could be ruled invalid if a judge concludes that you were not of sound mind when you signed the durable power of attorney, or that you were the victim of fraud or undue influence. The power of attorney could also be invalidated for a technical error, such as the failure to have your document notarized. If that happens, the judge could appoint a conservator to take over management of your property.

Physician's Determination of Incapacity

I, ___Jennifer Frank_____,

of the City of ___Orange_____, County of ___Orange_____,

State of California, declare under penalty of perjury that:

1. I am a physician licensed to practice in the state of California.

2. I examined ___Alice Murphy_____

    on ___October 12_____, ___2004__. It is my professional opinion that

    ___Alice Murphy_____

    is currently incapacitated and unable to manage his/her finances and property.

Dated: ___October 12, 2004_____

___*Jennifer Frank*_____
Signature of Physician

___Jennifer Frank_____, Physician

Certificate of Acknowledgment of Notary Public

State of California

County of _____ } ss

On _____, _____, before me, _____,

personally appeared _____,

personally known to me (or proved on the basis of satisfactory evidence) to be the person whose name is

subscribed to the within instrument, and acknowledged to me that he or she executed the same in his or her

authorized capacity and that by his or her signature on the instrument, the person, or the entity upon behalf

of which the person acted, executed the instrument.

WITNESS my hand and official seal.

_____

Notary Public for the State of California

[NOTARY SEAL]   My commission expires _____

If a court appoints a conservator, the agent becomes accountable to the conservator—not just to you—and the conservator has the power to revoke your durable power of attorney if the court approves. (Cal. Prob. Code § 4206.)

c. You Get Divorced

In California, if your spouse is your agent and you divorce, your ex-spouse's authority is immediately terminated. (Cal. Prob. Code § 4154(a).) If you named an alternate (successor) agent in your power of attorney, that person takes over as agent. However, if you get divorced it's best to revoke your durable power of attorney and make a new one.

If you are a member of a registered domestic partnership and your partnership ends, the law doesn't automatically revoke your partner's authority under a power of attorney for finances. Be sure to revise your document if you want a new agent.

d. No Agent Is Available

A durable power of attorney must end if there's no one to serve as the agent. To avoid this, you can name an alternate agent who will serve if your first choice can't. (See Section B4.)

For a bit of extra insurance, you can also allow the alternate agent to choose someone else to take over, if it's ever necessary. (See Section B4.)

e. After Your Death

A durable power of attorney ends when the principal dies. However, if the agent doesn't know of your death and continues to act on your behalf, those actions are still valid. (Cal. Prob. Code § 4152(b).)

If you want your agent to have any authority over winding up your affairs after your death, you must grant that authority in your will or living trust. (See

the list of estate planning resources at the end of Chapter 1.)

4. How Much It Costs

In most instances, the only expense of creating a durable power of attorney is the price of this book and a few dollars for a notary to verify your signature on the document. In some situations, however, there may be other costs.

a. Up-Front Costs

If you give your agent power over your real estate, you'll need to file (record) your durable power of attorney with the county clerk's office. Recording your document is explained in Section D3, below. There is a small fee, about $7 for the first page plus a few dollars for each additional page.

Although it's not usually necessary, you may decide that you want a lawyer to review or modify your durable power of attorney. The fee for this service shouldn't be large, at least by lawyers' standards. You can expect to pay around $100 to have a lawyer review your document.

b. Ongoing Costs

If you become incapacitated and someone must handle your financial affairs for you, additional expenses will crop up. But if you have a durable power of attorney, the cost will be less than if a court-appointed conservator had to take over.

Agent's payment. If you decide your agent is to be paid for helping you, those fees will be paid from your assets. (For information about paying your agent, see Section B5.)

Fees for accountants and other experts. If the agent must hire professionals, such an accountant or finan-cial adviser, to help with managing your property and finances, their fees will be paid from your assets.

5. Will Your Power of Attorney Be Accepted?

Durable powers of attorney are common; financial institutions, insurance companies, and government agencies are used to them. Your agent, armed with a signed and notarized power of attorney document, should have no problem getting people to accept his or her authority.

If questions come up when an agent tries to take action under the power of attorney, the agent should be able to deal with them. Here are some issues third parties may raise:

Is the document still valid? It's reasonable for someone to want to make sure that your durable power of attorney hasn't been changed or revoked. As reassurance, your agent can show that person the power of attorney document; it clearly states that any person who receives a copy of the document may accept it without the risk of legal liability unless he or she knows that the document has been revoked.

And under California law, anyone who, in good faith, relies on a power of attorney that appears to be valid and properly executed can't be sued if the document later turns out to be invalid. (Cal. Prob. Code § 4303.)

Your agent can also sign a sworn statement (an affidavit) in front of a notary public, stating that as far as he or she knows, the durable power of attorney has not been revoked and that you are still alive. Under the law, this statement is sufficient to prove to third parties that the durable power of attorney is still valid. (Cal. Prob. Code § 4305.)

If a third party is unusually stubborn, the agent can point to Section 4406 of the California Probate Code, which states that a third party who receives a properly prepared statutory form power of attorney (the kind contained in this book), must honor the document under any circumstance in which the third party would be required to accept your own authority. In other words, if your bank is required to let you withdraw funds from an account, it can't refuse your agent's request to do the same when faced with a properly prepared document. If it does, Section 4406 allows your agent to get a court order requiring the bank to accept the power of attorney—and perhaps recover attorney's fees for the trouble.

Does the agent have the authority he or she claims? Any third party who relies on a durable power of attorney must be sure that the agent has the power he or she claims to have. That means the third party must examine the document, to see what power it grants.

California's power of attorney law is very specific about the agent's powers. For example, if you give your agent authority over your banking transactions, the document indicates this, and the California statutes describe in detail what the agent can do, including:

- managing, changing, or terminating accounts
- withdrawing funds by writing checks or other methods
- receiving bank statements
- obtaining or closing a safe deposit box and adding to or withdrawing from its contents
- borrowing money
- applying for credit cards, and
- changing the terms of bank loans.

If necessary, your agent can point to the statutory section that grants the power in question, so a doubting third party can read it in black and white. (The powers you can grant to your agent are defined in Sections 4451-4463 of the California Probate Code, and are discussed in detail in Section C4, below.)

An agent who runs into resistance should seek, politely but insistently, someone higher up in the bureaucracy. And, as mentioned above, the agent may want to point out the requirements of Probate Code Section 4406.

Were you of sound mind? If you weren't of sound mind when you signed your durable power, the document has no legal effect. (See Section A1, above.) If you think that someone might raise this issue later and demand proof that you knew what you were doing when you signed your durable power, you may want discuss your concerns with a lawyer as discussed in Chapter 1, Section D.

B. About Your Agent for Finances

This section explains more about the responsibilities the person you name as agent will have toward you and your property. It also offers some guidance to help you choose the right person for the job.

1. Powers You Can Grant

Commonly, people give an agent broad power over their finances. But you can give your agent as much or as little power as you wish. With the durable power of attorney form in this book, the powers you can give your agent include:

- using your assets to pay your everyday expenses and those of your family
- handling transactions with banks and other financial institutions
- buying, selling, maintaining, paying taxes on, and mortgaging real estate and other property
- filing and paying your taxes
- managing your retirement accounts
- collecting benefits from Social Security, Medicare, other government programs, or civil or military service
- investing your money in stocks, bonds, and mutual funds
- buying and selling insurance policies and annuities for you
- operating your small business
- claiming or disclaiming property you inherit
- hiring someone to represent you in court
- making gifts of your assets to organizations and individuals that you choose, and
- transferring property to a living trust you've already set up.

These powers are discussed in detail in Section C4.

You can also place conditions or restrictions upon the agent. For example, you can give your agent authority over your real estate, but with the express restriction that your house may not be sold.

2. What Your Agent Can't Do

There are a few powers you can't give to your agent under your durable power of attorney for finances.

Medical Decisions. A durable power of attorney for finances does not give your agent legal authority to make health care decisions for you. To make sure that your wishes for medical care are known and followed, you should create medical directives. (See Chapters 2 and 3.)

Marriage, Adoption, Voting, Wills. You cannot authorize your agent to marry, adopt, vote in public elections, or make a will on your behalf. These acts are considered too personal to delegate to someone else.

Powers You've Already Delegated. If you've already given someone legal authority to manage some or all of your property, you cannot delegate that authority to your agent. Here are two common examples:

- You created a living trust that gives the successor trustee power over trust property if you become incapacitated. (See Chapter 1, Section C1.)
- You signed a partnership agreement that gives your partners authority to manage your interest in the business if you can't.

3. Legal Responsibilities

How much authority you want to give your agent is up to you. But whatever the agent's duties, he or she must always act in your best interests.

a. Basic Responsibilities: Honesty and Prudence

The agent you appoint in your power of attorney is a "fiduciary"—someone who holds a position of trust and must act in your best interests. Essentially, the law requires your agent to:

- handle your property honestly and prudently
- act in your best interests
- keep your property completely separate from his or her own
- keep you informed and follow your instructions as much as possible under the circumstances
- keep adequate records
- use any special skills that the agent has, and
- deliver your property to the appropriate people when the agent's authority ends.

These legal responsibilities do not present problems in most simple situations. For example, if you just want your agent to sign for your pension check, deposit it in your bank account, and pay for your basic needs, there is slight possibility of uncertainty or dispute.

Sometimes, however, these rules impose unnecessary hardships on an agent. For example, your property may already be mixed with that of your agent, and it may make good sense for that to continue. Fortunately, you can use your power of attorney document to give your agent permission to deviate from some of the rules.

These rules and exceptions are discussed below.

(1) Managing Your Property Prudently

The agent must be careful with your money and other property. California law generally requires an agent to act as a "prudent person" would under the circumstances. (Cal. Prob. Code § 4231(a).) That means the agent has no obligation to make canny investment moves with your cash. The primary goal is not to lose your money.

The agent may, however, take careful actions on your behalf. For example, if your money is in a low-interest bank account, the agent might invest it in government bonds, which pay higher interest but are still very safe.

As long as your agent is not paid to act for you (most agents are spouses, partners, close relatives, or friends who are not compensated for their services), the agent is not liable for a well-meaning decision that turned out badly. (Cal. Prob. Code § 4231(b).) The agent will be held personally responsible for losses only if he or she is extremely careless with your assets or actually steals from you.

However, some agents may be held to a higher standard than that of a "prudent person." If your agent has special skills or expertise—for example, if she is a lawyer or an accountant—she is required to meet the standard of care that would be expected of anyone with her skills. A certified financial planner, for instance, will be expected to perform at the level of other financial planners, not at that of ordinary folks without the same expertise. (Cal. Prob. Code § 4231(c).)

(2) Acting in Your Best Interests

When taking action under a power of attorney, California law requires your agent to act solely in your interest and to avoid conflicts of interest. An agent who is acting according to your best interests, however, is not forbidden from benefiting personally from a transaction conducted on your behalf. (Cal. Prob. Code § 4232.)

EXAMPLE: David is the agent for his elderly mother, Irene. After Irene's failing eyesight makes it impossible for her to drive, David decides to sell her car for her and put the money in a certificate of deposit at her bank. After thinking it over, David decides that his family could use another car for their teenage daughter. He looks up the car's current market value to make sure he is paying a fair amount, writes a check, and opens the CD in his mother's name. Finally, he transfers ownership of the vehicle to his daughter.

This transaction is most likely acceptable under California law, because David undertakes the transaction primarily to benefit his mother.

Even though California law is somewhat flexible in allowing the agent to benefit personally from transactions conducted under a power of attorney, doing so has the potential to put your agent on shaky ground if someone challenges these actions in court. Activities that create conflicts of interest (or that give the impression of such conflicts) between the principal and agent are called "self-dealing"—and they are likely to draw scrutiny from a court in the event of a dispute about how the agent is handling the principal's affairs. For this reason, it's generally best for agents to avoid self-dealing altogether.

Nevertheless, in some circumstances it makes sense for the agent to have permission to benefit from transactions carried out under a power of attorney—for example, if the agent is your spouse, a close family member, a business partner, or other person whose affairs are already intertwined with yours. For instance, if your agent is also your wife, or your child who will someday inherit most or all of your property, you don't want her to have to worry because selling an item of property you own jointly will benefit her as well as you. In a case like this, you can provide extra protection for your agent by adding a simple clause to your power of attorney that explicitly allows the agent to benefit from transactions conducted on your behalf. (See Section C5.)

(3) Keeping Funds Separate

An agent is not allowed to mix (commingle) your funds with his or her own. (Cal. Prob. Code § 4233.) However, if you wish, your power of attorney can specifically authorize your agent to commingle funds. You will probably want to grant this authority if you appoint your spouse or partner as agent, and your finances are already thoroughly mixed together in joint bank or security accounts.

> **EXAMPLE:** Jim and Eduardo have been living together for 25 years. They have a joint checking account and share all basic living expenses. Each names the other as his agent in durable power of attorney documents. To avoid any possible problems, Jim and Eduardo both include, in their powers of attorney, specific provisions that allow commingling of funds.

Different Powers for Alternate Agents

Even if you want to give your first-choice agent full power to benefit personally from transactions conducted on your behalf, or to mix your funds with his or hers, you may not feel comfortable giving an alternate agent the same authority. This may be the case if you name your spouse or partner as agent and then name an alternate with whom you are not so closely or financially entwined. In your power of attorney form, you can give your alternate agent the same power as your first choice, or restrict the alternate's authority when it comes to personal benefit and mixing funds. (See Section C5.)

---

(4) Keeping You Informed and Following Your Instructions

Even after you are incapacitated, your agent must do as much as is reasonable to keep in contact with you and to follow whatever wishes you express about how you want your finances handled. An agent who feels that your judgment is so impaired that your directions are not in your own best interests can ask a court to grant permission to disobey your wishes. (Cal. Prob. Code § 4234.)

(5) Keeping Good Records

Your agent is legally required to keep accurate and separate records for all transactions made on your behalf. (Cal. Prob. Code § 4236(a).) This is true whether or not the agent is paid to serve as agent. (Paying your agent is discussed in Section B5, below.) Good records are particularly important if the agent ever wants to resign and turn the responsibility over to a successor.

Record keeping isn't an onerous requirement. All the agent must be able to do is show where and how your money has been spent. In most instances, it's enough to have a balanced checkbook and receipts for bills paid and claims made. And because the agent will probably file tax returns on your behalf, income and expense records may be necessary.

You and your prospective agent should discuss and agree on what record keeping is appropriate. The agent may also want to review your current records now to find out where they're kept and make sure they're in order. If you don't have clear records, the agent may have to spend a lot of time sorting things out later.

As part of managing your finances, the agent may hire a bookkeeper, accountant, or other financial advisor and pay for the services from your property.

Nolo's Personal RecordKeeper. If, like many people, your records are in haphazardly labeled shoeboxes and file folders, this may be a good time to get organized. One way to start is with *Nolo's Personal RecordKeeper*, a computer program that helps you organize family, medical, financial, and insurance records and inventory your property.

Making Reports

Your agent is not required to provide accountings or reports of transactions made on your behalf unless the power of attorney document requires reports (see Section C5) or one of the following people requests or orders a report:

- you
- your conservator, if a court appoints one for you
- your personal representative (executor), if you die with a will
- anyone who stands to inherit property from you, if you die without a will, or
- a court.

(Cal. Prob. Code § 4236(b).) The people on this list may also examine and copy any records kept by the agent that relate to the power of attorney. (Cal. Prob. Code § 4236(c).)

---

(6) Using Special Skills

An agent who has any special skills—say your agent happens to be a securities broker or real estate agent—must apply those skills to their full extent when acting on your behalf. (Cal. Prob. Code § 4237.)

(7) Turning Over Your Property

When the agent's authority ends, he or she is required to promptly deliver your property to the appropriate people. (Cal. Prob. Code § 4238(a).) If you are not incapacitated at the time—for example, if you revoke the durable power while you are still of sound mind —this means returning property to you or doing with it whatever you direct. If you are incapacitated, delivering your property may mean giving control to:

- a successor agent
- your spouse, if the property is community property
- a conservator, if one has been appointed, or
- your personal representative (executor), after your death.

If the person taking control of the property requests it, the agent is also required to deliver copies of any transaction records related to the property. (Cal. Prob. Code § 4238(b).)

b. Supervision of the Agent

An agent is not directly supervised by a court; that's the whole point of appointing one. The agent is not required to file reports with any courts or government agencies unless ordered to do so (see "Making Reports," just above).

If you make a durable power of attorney and become incapacitated, a court may become involved only if someone close to you fears that the agent is acting dishonestly or not in your best interests. It's rare, but close relatives or friends may ask a court to order the agent to take certain actions. Or they may ask the court to terminate the power of attorney and appoint a conservator to look after your affairs. (As mentioned earlier, if a conservator is appointed for you, the agent will have to account to the conservator—or the conservator may get court approval to revoke the durable power of attorney altogether.) Disgruntled family members or friends may also challenge the durable power of attorney, on the grounds that you weren't of sound mind when you signed it or were the victim of some kind of fraud.

California law specifically authorizes anyone who is concerned to ask a court to resolve questions about a power of attorney, including whether the document is valid or whether the agent is acting properly under it. (Cal. Prob. Code §§ 4540, 4541.)

c. Resignation

No one can be forced to serve as an agent—it's a voluntary job, and in theory, the agent can resign at any time. (Cal. Prob. Code § 4207.) Resignation is simplest when the durable power names a successor to take over as agent, and the successor is willing and able to serve.

If your agent resigns after you are incapacitated and your document doesn't name a successor, or the successor cannot serve, a conservatorship proceeding may be necessary. (See Chapter 1, Section

A3.) In some circumstances, leaving a disabled principal in the lurch could be considered a breach of duty, and a court might order an agent to continue serving until a conservator is appointed and takes over. (Cal. Prob. Code § 4541.)

4. Choosing Your Agent

The most important decision you must make when you create a financial power of attorney is who will serve as your agent.

Depending on the powers you grant, the agent may have tremendous power over your property. You need to choose someone you trust completely. Fortunately, most of us know at least one such person —usually a spouse, partner, relative, or close friend. Or, perhaps one member of your family is particularly good at managing business affairs and routinely helps you and other family members with them. If there's no one you trust completely with this great authority, a financial power of attorney isn't for you.

Remember that no one will be keeping an eye on the agent. If your agent handles your affairs carelessly or dishonestly while you are incapacitated, the only recourse of your family or friends would be a lawsuit—obviously, not a satisfactory approach. Lawsuits are burdensome and expensive, and would entangle your loved ones in all the legal red tape a power of attorney is designed to avoid. And there's no guarantee that money lost by a bungling agent would ever be recovered. All this is not said to frighten you needlessly, but simply to underscore the need to make a careful choice about who will represent you.

If you are of sound mind, you can always "fire" a troublesome or dishonest agent by revoking the power of attorney document. But choosing wisely from the start will help you avoid both hard feelings and monetary losses.

a. General Considerations

Any adult can serve as your agent. But don't appoint someone without first discussing the job with that person and making sure he or she accepts this serious responsibility.

In most situations, the agent does not need extensive experience in financial management; common sense, dependability, and complete honesty are enough. If necessary, your agent can get professional help—from an accountant, lawyer, or tax preparer, perhaps—and pay for it out of your assets. If, however, you want the agent to help run your small business or manage extensive investments, be sure you choose someone with enough experience to handle the job.

It's also a good idea to name someone who lives nearby, if possible. Your agent will be responsible for taking care of the day-to-day details of your finances: opening mail, paying bills, looking after property, and so on. Of course, many families are spread across the country these days. If there's only one person you trust enough to name as agent and that person lives far away, you may have to settle for the less than ideal situation.

Sometimes it's tough to know whom to choose. Perhaps your mate is ill or wouldn't be a good choice for other reasons. Or you may not know anyone whom you feel entirely comfortable asking to take over your financial affairs. Or, if you have an active, complex investment portfolio or own a business, you might decide that your agent needs business skills, knowledge, or management abilities beyond those of the people closest to you.

If you're not sure whom to choose, read the rest of this section and discuss the issue with those close to you. It's better not to make a power of attorney than to entrust your affairs to someone in whom you don't have complete confidence.

Family conflicts can disrupt the handling of your affairs. Long-standing feuds among family members may result in objections to your choice of agent or the extent of the authority you delegate. This can wreak havoc with your agent's ability to handle tasks for you. If you foresee such personal conflicts, it's wise to try to defuse them in advance. A discussion with the people who are leery of the power of attorney might help. If you still feel uncomfortable after talking things over, you may want to discuss the troubles with a knowledgeable lawyer. A lawyer can review your estate planning documents and might help you feel reassured that your plans will be carried out as you wish.

b. If You're Married

If you're married, you'll probably want to make your spouse your agent unless there is a compelling reason not to. There are powerful legal and practical reasons, in addition to the emotional ones, for appointing your spouse. The main one is that naming anyone else creates the risk of conflicts between the agent and your spouse over how to manage property that belongs to both spouses. (Your spouse's authority over your property, if you become incapacitated, is discussed in Chapter 1, Section C1.)

> **EXAMPLE:** Henry and Amelia, a married couple, each create a durable power of attorney for finances. Henry names Amelia as his agent, but Amelia names her sister Anna. Later, Amelia becomes unable to manage her affairs, and Anna takes over as her agent. Soon Anna and Henry are arguing bitterly over what should be done with the house and investments that Henry and Amelia own together. If they can't resolve their differences, Henry or Anna may have to go to court and ask a judge to determine what is in Amelia's best interests.

If your spouse is ill, quite elderly, or simply not equipped to manage your financial affairs, you may have to name someone else as agent. The wisest course is for you and your spouse to agree on who the agent should be, perhaps one of your grown children.

Remember that if your spouse is your agent, that designation automatically ends if you get divorced. (Cal. Prob. Code § 4154(a).) After a divorce you should revoke your power of attorney and create a new one, naming someone else as your new agent.

c. If You Make an Advance Health Care Directive

To name someone who will make medical decisions on your behalf, you must prepare an advance health care directive (see Chapter 3). It's usually a good idea to name the same person as both your agent for finances and your agent for health care under your advance directive. If that's not practical for some reason, make sure you name agents who get along well and will be able to work together; they may have to do so often. For example, if you need medical care, your health care agent will have to turn to your financial agent to be sure insurance matters are handled and medical bills are paid.

Many Jobs, One Agent	
Naming the same person for the following jobs will help to ensure that decisions are made for you with a minimum of confusion and interference.	
Job	**Duties**
Agent under your durable power of attorney for finances	Manages your finances if you are incapacitated.
Agent under your advance directive for health care	Directs your health care if you are incapacitated. If you choose, your health care agent also decides where you will live and handles the disposition of your body after your death.
Executor of your will (called your "personal representative" in California)	Winds up your affairs after your death, including paying debts and distributing property to the people who inherit it.
Successor trustee of your living trust, if you have one	Manages trust property if you become incapacitated and distributes it after your death.

d. If You Have a Living Trust

If you have created a revocable living trust to avoid probate or minimize estate taxes, the "successor trustee" you named in the trust document will have power over the trust property if you become incapacitated. Or, if you and your spouse made a living trust together, the trust document almost certainly gives your spouse authority over trust property if you become incapacitated. (Living trusts are discussed in Chapter 1, Section C1.)

Creating a financial power of attorney doesn't change any of this. Your agent will not have authority over property held in your living trust. To avoid conflicts, it's advisable to have the same person managing both trust property and nontrust property if you become incapacitated. So normally, you'll name the same person as successor trustee and as your agent.

> **EXAMPLE:** Carlos, a widower, prepares a revocable living trust to avoid probate and a durable power of attorney for finances in case he becomes incapacitated. He names his son, Jeffrey, as both successor trustee of the living trust and agent under the durable power of attorney.
>
> Several years later, Carlos has a stroke and is temporarily unable to handle his everyday finances. Jeffrey steps in to deposit his father's pension checks and pay his monthly bills, using his authority as agent. As successor trustee, he also has legal authority over the property Carlos holds in his living trust, including Carlos's house.

e. Appointing More Than One Person

In general, it's a bad idea to name more than one agent, because conflicts between them could disrupt the handling of your finances. Also, some banks and other financial institutions prefer to deal with a single agent.

If you're tempted to name more than one person simply so that no one feels hurt or left out, think again. It may be better to pick one person for the job and explain your choice to your loved ones now. If you name more than one person and they don't get along, they may wind up resolving their disputes in court. This might result in more bad feelings than if you had just picked one person to be agent, and explained your choice, in the first place.

(1) How Multiple Agents Make Decisions

If you name more than one agent, you'll have to grapple with the question of how they should make their decisions. You can require co-agents to carry out their duties in one of two ways:

- they must all agree before they take any action on your behalf, or
- they may make decisions independent of one another.

Both methods have strengths and pitfalls. Requiring your agents to act jointly ensures that decisions are made carefully and with the knowledge of everyone involved, but coordinating multiple decision makers can be burdensome and time consuming. On the other hand, allowing your agents to act separately makes it easy to get things done, but allowing more than one person to make independent decisions about your finances can lead to poor record keeping and general confusion. For example, one agent could independently take money out of your bank accounts or sell stock without full knowledge of what the other is doing to manage your investments.

There's no hard-and-fast rule on which strategy is better. Choose the method that feels most comfortable to you.

(2) If Your Agents Disagree

If your agents get into a dispute that interferes with their ability to represent you properly, they may need help working things out. Getting help could mean hiring a mediator—or going to court to have a judge decide what's best. Your agents can decide how to handle the matter, keeping in mind that their foremost responsibility is to act in your best interest. The downside of all this is not just that there could be confusion and delays in handling your finances, but also that you'll probably be the one to pay the costs of settling the dispute.

(3) If One or More of Your Agents Can't Serve

If you name more than one agent, and one of them can't serve, the others will continue to serve. If none of them can serve, an alternate can take over. (See Subsection g, below, for more information about naming an alternate agent.)

f.   If You Can't Think of Anyone to Name

If you can't come up with a family member or close friend to name, you may want to consider asking your lawyer, business partner, or banker to serve as agent. If you really know and trust the person, it may be a good option for you. Otherwise, it's better not to make a power of attorney.

Don't name an institution, such as a bank, as agent. Though California law permits it, it's definitely not desirable. Serving as agent is a personal responsibility, and there should be personal connection and trust between you and your agent. If the person you trust most happens to be your banker, appoint that person, not the bank.

g.   Naming an Alternate Agent

It's a good idea to name someone who will take over as your agent in case your first choice can't serve or needs to resign after serving for a period of time. Your alternate will take over if your initial choice can't serve.

When naming an alternate, use the same criteria that you used to make your first choice for agent. Your alternate should be every bit as trustworthy and competent. If you don't know anyone you trust well enough, skip the matter altogether.

If You Name More Than One Agent

If you name more than one agent, the person you name as alternate will take over only if all of your agents must give up the job. If any of your first choices can continue to serve, they may do so alone, without the addition of your alternate.

As a further precaution, you can authorize your agent to appoint someone to serve if those you named cannot. You do this by giving your agent permission to delegate tasks to others. (See Section C5.) Allowing your agent to delegate authority to someone else eliminates the minimal risk that the position might become vacant because of the original agent's death, disability, or resignation. If this occurs, and you haven't named an alternate or your alternate is not available, your power of attorney would be useless. If you were incapacitated, there would have to be a court action, such as a full-scale conservatorship proceeding, to find someone to manage your affairs.

5.   Paying Your Agent

Under California law, an agent is entitled to reasonable compensation and to reimbursement for reasonable expenses incurred on your behalf. (Cal. Prob. Code § 4204.) However, in family situations, an agent is normally not paid if the duties won't be complicated or burdensome.

If, on the other hand, your property and finances are extensive, and the agent is likely to devote significant time and effort to managing them, compensation may be fair—and you can probably afford it. (Keep in mind, however, that an agent who is paid is also held to a higher standard of care when looking after your finances; see Section B3, above.) You should discuss and resolve the issue of payment with the proposed agent before you finalize your document.

If you decide to pay your agent, it's wise to specify the payment arrangement in your power of attorney form. (See Section C5 shows you how to do this.) You can set your own rate—for example, $10,000 per year, $10 per hour, or some other figure that you and your agent agree on. Or, if you don't want to decide on an amount right now, you can allow your agent to determine a reasonable wage if it seems appropriate. No single strategy works best for everyone. Choose the approach—and the amount—that feels right to you.

EXAMPLE 1: Frederick is quite wealthy. He owns and operates a successful chain of convenience stores in a large city. He also owns a house, several pieces of investment property, and a wide array of stocks. When he is diagnosed with a life-threatening illness, he creates a durable power of attorney appointing his close friend Barbara as his agent. Because he expects Barbara to watch over his business as well as tend to his other financial affairs, he feels it's appropriate to pay her for her services. Frederick and Barbara settle on a rate of $15,000 per year for her services.

EXAMPLE 2: Martin creates a springing durable power of attorney naming his brother, Andrew, as agent. Martin owns a complex investment portfolio, and the brothers agree that Andrew should be paid if he has to manage Martin's finances. They consider an hourly wage, but decide not to be that specific now. In his durable power of attorney, Martin states that Andrew may pay himself reasonable fees for his services if they're ever necessary.

If You Name More Than One Agent

If you name more than one agent and you want to pay them, your document will specify that each is to receive the same amount—for example, $5,000 per year or $12 per hour. If you allow your agents to determine a reasonable amount for their services, each will set his or her own salary.

C. Preparing Your Durable Power of Attorney

California provides a fill-in-the-blanks durable power of attorney form called the "Uniform Statutory Form Power of Attorney." It's called a "statutory form" because you can find the exact text of the form in the California statutes (Section 4401 of the California Probate Code). This type of form is also known as a

"short form" because the form itself doesn't include all the details of the authority granted to the agent. Instead, the form lists 13 broad powers (discussed in detail below). You choose the powers you want your agent to have; the details of each are spelled out in the California statutes. (Cal. Prob. Code §§ 4451-4463.)

The California statutory form is fairly straightforward and easy to complete. This section takes you through the form step by step and shows you a completed sample.

1. Getting Started

This book contains the California statutory power of attorney form on CD-ROM and as a tear-out form in Appendix B. If you use the CD-ROM, just use your word processor to complete and customize your form, following the instructions below.

If you use the tear-out version, start by making a few photocopies of the blank form. You can use one for a draft and save a clean one for the final document—the one you will sign and have notarized. It's best to complete the tear-out form using a typewriter (if you can find one), though filling in the blanks by hand is legally permissible. If you must hand print your document, print legibly and use black ink.

Your completed form should not contain any words that have been erased or whited out. If the instructions tell you to cross out something, type a string of x's through the words or draw a straight line through them.

Making a custom document with the CD-ROM. You will find it easier to customize your form if you use the CD-ROM at the back of the book; this is especially true if you want to add quite a few of the special instructions discussed in Section C5, below. (The printed statutory form provides a relatively small space for additional instructions. If you run out of room, you'll have to retype the entire form.) If you want to make a custom form using the CD, choose the file DPAF. Then type the clauses you want into the special instructions section of the form.

Get help if you need it. A durable power of attorney can transfer tremendous power either now or, in the case of a springing power of attorney, sometime in the future. Even though you can revoke your document at any time (as long as you are of sound mind), never create a durable power of attorney unless you thoroughly understand what you are doing. If you have questions, see an expert.

2. Your Name and Address

In the first blank on the form, enter your name and residence address. Enter your name as it appears on official documents such as your driver's license, bank accounts, or real estate deeds. This may or may not be the name on your birth certificate. Enter it first, middle (if you choose), then last.

> **EXAMPLE:** Your birth certificate lists your name as Rose Ellen Green. But you've always gone by Ellen and always sign documents as Ellen McNee, your married name. You should use Ellen McNee on your durable power of attorney.

Be sure to enter all names in which you hold bank accounts, stocks, bonds, real estate, and other property. This will make things far easier for your agent. If you're including more than one name, enter your full legal name first, followed by "aka" (also known as). Then enter your other names.

Making Your Records Consistent

If you use more than one name and you're up for some extra work, consider settling on one name, entering it on your power of attorney form and then changing your other documents to conform. This will clean up your records and save your agent some trouble later on. To change your name on official document and records—for example, bank accounts, deed, or Social Security records—you'll have to contact the appropriate government office or financial institution to find out what documentation they'll need to make the change for you.

3. Naming Your Agent

In the second blank, after the word "appoint," insert the name and address of the person (or people) who will serve as your agent for finances. (A reminder: It's almost always a bad idea to name more than one agent. See Section B4, above.)

It's also a good idea to name an alternate agent in case your first choice can't serve. You must use the "Special Instructions" part of the form to name an alternate. (See Section C5, below.)

4. Granting Powers to Your Agent

The next section of the form lists 13 powers. You can give your agent all of them or only some. Either way, you can put specific limitations on the powers that you grant. For example, if you give your agent authority over your real estate, you can still add special instructions forbidding the agent from selling your residence.

Scanning the list of powers, you may think it's not necessary to grant some of them—after all, why give your agent authority over "claims and litigation" when you aren't involved in any lawsuits? What you should keep in mind is that even though you aren't involved in a lawsuit now, you could be later. For example, your power of attorney might spring into effect because you're in the hospital, seriously injured in a car accident, and you can't take care of your financial affairs. Your agent might need authority to settle a claim on your behalf.

If you, like most people, want to give your agent every power on the list, initial the blank in front of line (N) and skip to the "Special Instructions" part of the form. (See Section C5, below.) If you want to give only some powers, initial the blank in front of each power you want to grant. You can cross out the others, but it's not required.

The rest of this section discusses and describes each power in turn. (They are lettered as they appear in the form itself.) It describes the actions that agents commonly take under the powers and flags anything about a power that might seem extreme or cause concern—for example, the agent's ability to change beneficiary designations under your retirement plans. This should help you understand the powers and decide which ones you feel comfortable giving to your agent.

More details about the agent's powers. This section doesn't cover every possible kind of action your agent could take under each power. Each of the powers is described in greater (and sometimes excruciating) detail in Sections 4451-4463 of the California Probate Code.

(A) Real Property Transactions

This power puts the agent in charge of managing any real estate you own. Your agent must, for example, pay your mortgage and taxes (with your assets) and arrange for necessary repairs and maintenance. Most important, the agent may sell, mortgage, partition, or lease your real estate.

The agent may also take any other action connected to real estate. For example, your agent may:

- buy or lease real estate for you
- refinance your mortgage to get a better interest rate
- pay off liens (legal claims) on your property
- buy insurance for your property
- build, remodel, or remove structures on your property
- grant easements over your property
- bring or defend lawsuits over real estate.

Remember, however, that the agent has a legal obligation to take only those actions that are in your best interests.

(B) Tangible Personal Property Transactions

Tangible personal property means physical items— for example, cars, furniture, jewelry, computers, and stereo equipment. It does not include real estate or intangible kinds of property such as stocks or bank notes. If you grant this power, your agent can buy, sell, rent, or exchange personal property on your behalf. Your agent can also insure, use, move, store,

repair, or pawn your personal things. Again, all actions must be taken in your best interest.

EXAMPLE: Paul names his wife, Gloria, as his agent for financial matters. When he later goes into a nursing home, his old car, which he can no longer use, becomes an expense Gloria cannot afford. As Paul's agent, she has legal authority to sell the car and use the proceeds to help take care of him.

(C) Stock and Bond Transactions

This power gives your agent the power to buy, sell, or exchange securities for you, including stocks, bonds, mutual funds, certificates of deposit, and almost all other financial instruments. (The exceptions are commodity fixtures contracts and call-and-put options on stocks or stock indexes.) Your agent can buy or sell securities on your behalf, accept or transfer certificates or other evidence of ownership, and exercise voting rights.

Brokers may have their own power of attorney forms. Many brokerage houses have their own power of attorney forms. If yours does, it's a good idea to use it in addition to your statutory power of attorney. Using your broker's form will make things easier for your agent because your broker will have no need to investigate your power of attorney or quibble over its terms. The broker will already have its form on file and will understand exactly what your agent is authorized to do.

(D) Commodity and Option Transactions

Most folks aren't involved in commodity trading, but if you are, this power lets your agent buy, sell, exchange, assign, settle, or exercise options and commodities, and set up, manage, or terminate option accounts with a broker. It gives your agent the power to handle commodity futures contracts and stock call-and-put options traded on a regulated option exchange.

(E) Banking and Other Financial Institution Transactions

One of the most common reasons for making a power of attorney is to arrange for someone to handle banking transactions. If you give your agent authority to handle your bank accounts, your bills can be paid, and pension or other checks can be deposited in your accounts even if you are not able to take care of these matters yourself.

> **EXAMPLE:** Virginia, who is in her 70s, is admitted to the hospital for emergency surgery. She's too weak to even think about paying her bills or depositing her Social Security check—and anyway, she can't get to the bank. Fortunately, she earlier created a durable power of attorney for finances, naming her niece Marianne as her agent. Marianne can deposit Virginia's Social Security benefits and sign checks to pay the bills that come while Virginia is in the hospital.

Your agent may open and close accounts with banks, savings and loans, credit unions, or other financial institutions on your behalf. The agent may write checks on these accounts, endorse checks you receive, and receive account statements. The agent also has access to your safe deposit box, to withdraw or add to its contents. He or she may also borrow money on your behalf, and pledge your assets as security for the loan.

Signing Checks and Other Documents

Many people wonder how the agent signs checks and other documents on behalf of the principal. Exact procedures vary depending on the financial institution or government agency. Typically, however, after visiting or contacting a particular institution or agency to establish his or her authority, the agent will first sign your name and then his or her own name to checks and documents, followed by words such as "under power of attorney dated June 15, 2002" or simply, "POA."

⚠ Ask your financial institutions about their power of attorney forms. Many banks and other financial institutions have their own power of attorney forms. Even though granting the banking power will give your agent authority to act on your behalf at any financial institution, it's a good idea to use the financial institution's form in addition to the statutory form. Using the form that your financial institution is most familiar with may make it easier for your agent to get things done.

(F) Business Operating Transactions

This power gives your agent authority to act for you in operating a business that you own yourself or that you run with other people. Subject to the terms of any partnership agreement, limited liability company operating agreement, or corporate rules (bylaws and shareholders' agreements), your agent may:

- sell or liquidate the business
- merge with another company
- prepare, sign, and file reports, information, and returns with government agencies
- pay business taxes
- enforce the terms of a partnership agreement, if any, in court
- exercise any power or option you have under a partnership agreement.

If your business is a sole proprietorship, the agent may also:

- hire and fire employees
- move the business
- change the nature of the business or its methods of operation, including selling, marketing, accounting, and advertising
- change the name of the business
- change the form of the business's organization —that is, enter into a partnership agreement or incorporate the business
- continue or renegotiate the business's contracts
- hire lawyers, accountants, or others

• collect and spend money on behalf of the business.

If you're a sole proprietor, a power of attorney is a very useful way to let someone else run the business if you're unable to do so, either for a short time or due to incapacity. Be sure to work out a business plan with the person you intend to appoint as your agent; explain what you want for your business and how you expect it to be managed.

If you operate your business with other people as a partnership, limited liability company, or closely held corporation, your business agreement should cover what happens if a partner or shareholder becomes unavailable. Typically, the other business owners can operate the business during your absence or even buy out your share. These rules can't be overridden by a power of attorney. So carefully check your partnership agreement, operating agreement, or corporate bylaws and shareholders' agreements.

> **EXAMPLE:** Mike wants his wife, Nancy, to be his agent to manage his finances if he becomes incapacitated. Mike, a house painter, runs the M-J Painting Company with his equal partner, Jack. Mike and Jack's partnership agreement provides that if one partner becomes incapacitated, the other has exclusive authority to operate the business.
>
> Mike, Jack, and Nancy should think through the arrangement carefully; if Jack and Nancy have conflicts over money, there could be problems. Whatever they decide on should be spelled out in detail in the partnership agreement. They may also want to create a customized durable power of attorney, with a lawyer's help, that sets out the details of the business arrangements.

(G) Insurance and Annuity Transactions

This power allows your agent to buy, borrow against, cash in, or cancel insurance policies or annuity contracts for you and your spouse, children, and other dependent family members. The agent's authority extends to all policies and contracts you own, whether they name you or someone else as the beneficiary. (Beneficiaries are the people who will receive the proceeds of the policy when you die.)

The one exception to this rule covers any insurance policies you own with your spouse. Under these policies, your spouse must consent to any transaction that affects the policy. So if your agent is not your spouse, he or she will have to obtain your spouse's permission before taking action. In California, a community property state (meaning that most property acquired during marriage belongs to both spouses), policies that are in one spouse's name may in fact be owned by both. If you have questions about who owns your insurance policies, consult a lawyer.

If you already have an insurance policy or annuity contract, your agent can keep paying the premiums or cancel it, whichever he or she decides is in your best interests.

Your agent is also permitted to name—or change—the beneficiaries of your insurance policies or annuity contracts. This is a broad power, and it's a good idea to discuss your wishes about it with your agent. If you don't want your agent to change your beneficiary designations, you should make that clear in the special instructions part of your form. (See Section C5, below.) If you have strong feelings about whom the beneficiary of any new policies should be, you can discuss that as well.

There is one important limitation on your agent's ability to designate beneficiaries. Your agent cannot name himself or herself as beneficiary on a renewal of, extension of, or substitute for an existing policy unless he or she was already the beneficiary before you signed the power of attorney.

(H) Estate, Trust, and Other Beneficiary Transactions

This power primarily authorizes your agent to act on your behalf to claim or disclaim (give up) property you inherit or are entitled to from any other source. But it also gives your agent the important power to transfer items of property into your living trust, if you have created one.

(1) Claiming or Disclaiming Property

If you are entitled to inherit property or receive money from another source—a trust fund, for example—your agent can make your claim for you. Or, if you don't really need the money, your agent could turn down the cash. (Of course, your agent can't turn away property you inherit unless he or she feels that it's in your best interest to do so.)

Your agent is also entitled to watch out for your interests with regard to the property you stand to receive. This means, for example, that the agent can initiate legal proceedings on your behalf to clarify your rights to the property or to question improper actions of whoever is in charge of the assets.

(2) Living Trust Transactions

A revocable living trust is a legal structure you create by preparing and signing a document that specifies who will receive certain property at your death. In this way, it operates much like a will. Unlike a will, however, property in a living trust avoids the cost and delay of probate. Certain kinds of trusts also help you save on estate taxes.

If you've already set up a revocable living trust to avoid probate or estate taxes, this power gives your agent the authority to transfer items of your property to that trust. But your agent can transfer an item of property into your trust only if you've given him or her authority over that kind of property elsewhere in your document. For example, if you want your agent to be able to transfer real estate into your living trust, you must also grant Power (A), which gives your agent full power over your real estate. Or, if you want your agent to have authority to transfer bank accounts to your living trust, you must also grant Power (E), the banking transactions power.

> **EXAMPLE:** Maureen sets up a revocable living trust to avoid probate at her death, and holds her house and some valuable antiques in the trust. She also makes a durable power of attorney for

finances. Years later, when Maureen becomes incapacitated from a stroke, her son Paul takes over as her agent. While she is incapacitated, Maureen inherits a house from her elder sister. Paul, as agent, is able to transfer the house to Maureen's living trust—avoiding a substantial probate bill for Maureen's heirs when she dies.

(I) Claims and Litigation

This provision allows your agent to act for you in all matters that involve courts or government agencies. For example, your agent can bring or settle a lawsuit on your behalf. He or she can also accept court papers intended for you, and hire an attorney to represent you in court, if necessary. (Unless your agent is a lawyer, he or she may not actually represent you in court, but must hire someone to do so.) If you lose a lawsuit, the agent can use your assets to pay the winner whatever you are obligated to pay.

(J) Personal and Family Maintenance

This is an important power. It gives the agent the authority to use your assets to pay your everyday expenses and those of your family. The agent can spend your money for your family's food, living quarters, education, cars, medical and dental care, membership dues (for churches, clubs, or other organizations), vacations, and travel. The agent is allowed to spend as much as it takes to maintain your customary standard of living and that of your spouse, children, and anyone else you usually support.

You may normally support people other than your legal dependents. If you regularly take care of others—for example, you are the primary caretaker of a disabled sibling or an aging parent—your agent can use your assets to continue to help those people. You should talk with your agent and explain exactly what your support obligations are. If you like, you can write out specific guidelines in the special instructions part of your form. (See Section C5, below.)

(K) Benefits From Social Security, Medicare, Medicaid, or Other Governmental Programs, or Civil or Military Service

This power allows your agent to apply for, collect, and manage any government benefits you may be entitled to, from Social Security, Medicare, Medicaid, or other governmental programs, or from civil or military service. To collect most government benefits, your agent must send the government office a copy of the financial power of attorney. The Social Security Administration, however, requires more proof of authority. (See "Social Security Checks," below.)

Social Security Checks

To collect your Social Security benefits, your agent will have to take the power of attorney document to a local Social Security office. Someone there will interview the agent and establish him or her as your "representative payee"—that is, someone entitled to receive your Social Security checks for you.

If you're creating a power of attorney that's effective immediately, you can save your agent some work by simply contacting the Social Security Administration (SSA) now and naming your agent as your representative payee. However, that means your agent will start receiving your Social Security checks right away, and you may not want that. If it's not yet time for the agent to take control, you're better off granting the "government benefits" power and letting the agent deal with the Social Security Administration if the time comes.

In addition to granting the government benefits power, you might also consider having your Social Security check deposited directly into a bank account where your agent will have access to the funds without the hassles of dealing with the SSA. You can set up a direct deposit arrangement at any time, as long as you are of sound mind.

To appoint a representative payee or arrange for direct deposit of your benefits, contact the SSA at 800-772-1213.

(L) Retirement Plan Transactions

This power gives your agent authority over retirement plans such as pensions and IRAs. The agent may select payment options, designate beneficiaries (the people who will inherit any money left in the fund at your death) and change current beneficiary designations, make voluntary contributions to (and mandatory withdrawals from) your plan, change the way the funds are invested, and roll over plan benefits into other retirement plans. If authorized by the plan, the agent may make withdrawals, borrow from, sell assets to, and buy assets from the plan.

Be aware of how broad some of these powers are. For example, the power to change the beneficiaries of your retirement funds is a drastic one. You should talk with your agent to make your wishes clear with respect to this power.

(M) Tax Matters

This provision gives your agent authority to act for you in all state, local, federal, and foreign tax matters. The agent can prepare and file tax returns and other documents, pay tax you owe, contest tax bills, and collect refunds. (To file a tax return on your behalf, the agent must include a copy of the power of attorney with the return.) The agent is also authorized to receive confidential information from the IRS. (Cal. Prob. Code § 4235.)

The IRS Power of Attorney Form

The IRS has its own power of attorney form, but you don't need to use it. It is primarily designed to allow attorneys, accountants, and other professionals to receive confidential tax information on behalf of clients. It is not a comprehensive, durable power of attorney for tax matters. The power of attorney contained in this book gives your agent the power to receive confidential information from the IRS, plus the authority to handle any tax matters that arise.

5. Adding Special Instructions

Listed below are many clauses and powers that you might consider adding to the "Special Instructions" section of your durable power of attorney form. Certainly you won't need to use them all; you may not even need any. The most important clauses are the first two: naming an alternate agent and establishing the effective date if you wish to make a springing power of attorney. If you don't include this second provision, your durable power of attorney will take effect as soon as you sign it.

Possible Instructions

The special instructions you add to your form will depend on the particulars of your situation, so it would be impossible to cover every option in this book. This section discusses the types of instructions people are most likely to need:

- naming an alternate agent
- establishing the effective date of your power of attorney
- stating who will determine whether you are incapacitated
- paying your agent
- stating whether your agent may benefit personally under the document
- stating whether your agent may mix (commingle) his or her property with yours
- stating whether your agent may delegate duties to others
- granting additional powers to your agent, including the power to make gifts of your property, and the powers to create, modify, revoke, or fund a trust.
- placing limits on the agent's authority
- requiring the agent to make periodic reports to people that you choose
- nominating a conservator.

---

a. Alternate Agent

This clause permits you to name an alternate agent who will take over if your agent is unable to serve (see Section B4, above).

> If _____[name of agent]_____ does not or ceases to serve as agent, I appoint _____[name and address of alternate]_____ to serve as agent.

b. Effective Date and Determination of Incapacity

Use the following clause if you wish to make a durable power of attorney that doesn't take effect unless a doctor determines that you're incapacitated (see Section A2, above).

> This power of attorney shall take effect only if I become incapacitated or disabled and unable to manage my financial affairs.

If you include this clause, you should also use the following clause to name one or two doctors to determine whether or not you are incapacitated.

> For purposes of this durable power of attorney, my incapacity or disability shall be determined by the written declarations of _[insert correct number: "one" or "two"]_ licensed physician[s]. Each declaration shall be made under penalty of perjury and shall state that in the physician's opinion I am substantially unable to manage my financial affairs. No licensed physician shall be liable to me for any actions taken under this part that are done in good faith.

If you wish to name specific doctors to make the determination, add the following sentence to the end of the clause. If you don't use this sentence, your agent will choose the doctor(s) for you.

> If possible, the declaration[s] shall be made by _____[name of physician(s)]_____ .

c. Compensation and Reimbursement of Agent

You can choose any one of the following three clauses to provide reimbursement and compensation for your agent (see Section B5, above).

No Compensation; Reimbursement Only
My agent shall not be compensated for services, but shall be entitled to reimbursement, from my assets, for reasonable expenses incurred on my behalf. Reasonable expenses include but are not limited to reasonable fees for information or advice from accountants, lawyers, or investment experts relating to my agent's responsibilities under this power of attorney.

Reasonable Compensation to Be Determined by the Agent
My agent shall be entitled to reimbursement for reasonable expenses and reasonable compensation for services. What constitutes reasonable compensation shall be determined exclusively by my agent. If more than one agent is named in this document, each shall have the exclusive right to determine what constitutes reasonable compensation for his or her own duties.

Reasonable Compensation Stated in the Power of Attorney Document
My agent shall be entitled to reimbursement for reasonable expenses and compensation for services in the amount of $_____. If more than one agent is named in this document, each shall be entitled to receive this amount.

d. Personal Benefit by Agent

To make clear whether or not your agent is permitted to benefit personally from transactions conducted on your behalf, choose one of the following clauses. If you do not include any of them, your agent will be held to the standards discussed in Section B3, above.

Agent May Benefit Personally
My agent may buy any assets of mine or engage in any transaction he or she deems in good faith to be in my interest, no matter what the interest or benefit to my agent.

Primary Agent May Benefit Personally; Alternate Agent May Not
My agent may buy any assets of mine or engage in any transaction he or she deems in good faith to be in my interest, no matter what the interest or benefit to my agent. However, if an alternate agent is serving under this document, the alternate may not benefit personally from any transaction conducted on my behalf.

Agent May Not Benefit Personally
My agent may not benefit personally from any transaction conducted on my behalf.

If you give your agent the power to make gifts of your property to himself or herself (see Subsection g, below), but don't want the agent to benefit personally in any other way, you should add the following clause to your form:

Agent May Not Benefit Personally Except for Gifts
Although my agent may receive gifts of my property as described in this document, my agent may not benefit personally from any other transaction that he or she conducts on my behalf.

e. Commingling by Agent

You can choose one of the following clauses to specify your wishes about whether or not the agent may mix your funds with his or her own. If you don't use one of these clauses, the agent is not permitted to commingle funds. (See Section B3, above.)

Agent May Commingle Funds

My agent may commingle any of my funds with any funds of his or hers.

Primary Agent May Commingle Funds; Alternate Agent May Not

My agent may commingle any of my funds with any funds of his or hers. However, if an alternate agent is serving under this document, the alternate may not commingle any of my funds with his or hers.

f.   Delegation of Duties by Agent

If your agent resigns from the job and you named an alternate agent, that person will take over. But if there is no alternate available, or if your agent is only temporarily unavailable, the agent will need to find a stand-in. If you allow it, your agent can turn over all or part of his or her duties to someone else in this situation. This reassignment of duties is called "delegation."

An agent who is allowed to delegate tasks is free to turn over any or all of the job to a competent third person. This person may step in on a temporary basis or permanently, depending on the situation.

If you want to give your agent the power to delegate tasks, add the following clause to your form:

My agent may delegate, in writing, any authority granted under this power of attorney to a person he or she selects. Any such delegation shall state the period during which it is valid and specify the extent of the delegation.

If You Named More Than One Agent

Delegation becomes more complicated if you name more than one agent. Here are some issues to think about.

Agents Who Must Act Jointly

If you will require your agents to act together in all that they do (see Section C6, below), it's a good idea to give them the power to delegate responsibilities. That way, an agent who becomes temporarily unable to act on your behalf can delegate his or her authority to the remaining agents. Your remaining agents can use the written delegation to prove that they are permitted to act alone. If you don't grant the delegation power, an agent who will be unavailable will have to write and sign an affidavit—a sworn, notarized statement—saying that he or she cannot act for you. (An agent who permanently resigns can prepare a resignation form; the remaining agents can use that form to prove their authority.)

In the unlikely event that all of your agents will be temporarily unavailable, they can choose a person to take over if you've given them the power to delegate. Because your agents must act together, they must agree on any person who will take over some or all of their job.

Agents Who May Act Separately

If you've authorized your agents to act independently, allowing them to delegate tasks is probably not necessary or wise. The main reason for allowing delegation is to ensure that someone will always be on hand to take care of your finances. In your situation, if just one of your agents is temporarily unable to act on your behalf, the others may simply act alone, without any special documents or fuss. And you can name an alternate agent to take over if all of your agents must step down.

Allowing delegation in your situation could, in fact, create much unnecessary confusion. Because your agents may act independently, they could each delegate tasks to individuals that they choose— without consulting each other. When it comes to your finances, it's better not to open the door to that sort of chaos.

g. Gifts to Agent or Others

You may want your agent to be able to give away your property under some circumstances. On the other hand, allowing your agent to make gifts might feel like giving up too much control. This section helps you decide what makes sense for you.

If you give your agent the authority to make gifts, be sure to discuss your intentions with him or her. Your agent should have a sound understanding of your gift-giving goals, including the recipients you have in mind, under what circumstances gifts should be made, and in what amounts. Remember that any gifts your agent makes must be in your best interest or according to your explicit instructions.

(1) Allowing Your Agent to Make Gifts

There are many reasons why you might want to permit your agent to make gifts of your property. Here are a few of the most common.

Estate tax savings. Some people with very substantial assets set up a gift-giving plan aimed at reducing the amount of property they leave at death—and so shrinking their eventual estate tax liability. If you have set up this sort of plan, you'll probably want to authorize your agent to continue it. (This strategy may become obsolete, however, because of coming changes in estate tax law. For the latest, see the Wills & Estate Planning section of Nolo's online legal encyclopedia at www.nolo.com.)

Make sure your agent understands who should receive your property, how often, and in what amounts. You may want to explicitly limit the people and organizations to whom your agent may give gifts by listing them in your power of attorney document. (This is explained below.)

Other gift-giving plans. You may want to donate regularly to your church or a favorite charity. Or perhaps you've made a commitment to help a family member with college or starting up a business. Allowing your agent to make gifts means that these plans can go forward.

But again, talk with your agent and give as much guidance as you can. Remember that you can use your form to name the specific people and organizations to whom your agent may give your money or property.

Family emergencies. You may want your agent to be able to help out if a loved one is caught off guard by unexpected financial troubles. This is fine. But be sure your agent knows whom you'd want to help, what you consider an emergency, and what your limits are. Again, you may want to use your power of attorney form to limit the people to whom your agent can make gifts.

Gift Taxes

If your agent gives away more than a certain amount (currently $11,000) to any one person (except your spouse) or organization in one calendar year, a federal gift tax return will have to be filed. Gift tax may eventually have to be paid, but unless you give away or leave a very large amount of money, tax isn't usually paid until after your death. Making large gifts could put your agent in a bind. On one hand, your agent may feel that you would want to make a sizable gift—even if it's a taxable one—to a particular person or organization. On the other hand, making a taxable gift could increase the tax bill at your death.

For this reason, if you do permit your agent to make gifts, it's particularly important that you explain, ahead of time, what you intend, and what your limits are, if any.

(2) Gifts to the Agent

If you allow your agent to make gifts of your property, you must specifically decide whether or not your agent will be allowed to make gifts to himself or herself. This question raises some unique issues.

If you want to allow gifts to your agent, you must place an annual limit on those gifts. If you don't, *all* your property could be considered to legally belong to the agent if he or she dies before you do.

The sample clauses at the end of this section show you how to include the limit in your form. To avoid trouble with gift taxes, you may want to let the current gift tax threshold be your guide and set the limit at no more than $11,000. Whatever amount you choose, be sure it's far less than what you're worth. If you set the limit too high, you may in effect give everything to the agent.

Loan Forgiveness

When you give your agent the power to make gifts, you also give the power to forgive (cancel) debts owed to you. If anyone owes you money and you've authorized your agent to make gifts to them, be sure you let your agent know how you feel about those debts. Must they be paid, or may your agent forgive them under some circumstances?

If you authorize gifts to your agent and he or she owes you money, your agent can forgive those debts, too. But for these debts to you, your agent can't cancel an amount worth more than his or her maximum gift amount in any calendar year. For example, say your son, whom you've named as agent, owes you $20,000. You've placed the annual gift limit at $7,000. He can forgive his debt to you at the rate of $7,000 per year.

(3) Sample Clauses

Following are several sample clauses. You can include one of them in your form if you want to authorize your agent to make gifts of your property. Which one you should choose depends on whom you want to authorize to receive gifts, and on whether you want to name those people in your form. Remember, any gifts your agent makes must be in your best interest.

Your Agent May Make Gifts to People Other Than Himself or Herself

My agent may make gifts of my property, including forgiveness of debts owed to me and completion of charitable pledges that I have made. However, my agent shall not (i) appoint, assign, or designate any of my assets, interests, or rights directly or indirectly to himself or herself, or his or her estate or creditors, or the creditors of his or her estate, (ii) disclaim assets to which I would otherwise be entitled if the effect of the disclaimer is to cause the assets to pass directly or indirectly to my agent or his or her estate, or (iii) use my assets to discharge any of his or her legal obligations, including any obligation of support owed to others, excluding me and those I am legally obligated to support.

Your Agent May Make Gifts to Recipients That You List, but Not to Himself or Herself

My agent may make gifts of my property, including forgiveness of debts owed to me and completion of charitable pledges that I have made. However, the recipients of such gifts shall be limited to *[insert the names of people to whom your agent may make gifts, joined with "or"]* .

My agent shall not (i) appoint, assign, or designate any of my assets, interests, or rights directly or indirectly to himself or herself, or his or her estate or creditors, or the creditors of his or her estate, (ii) disclaim assets to which I would otherwise be entitled if the effect of the disclaimer is to cause such assets to pass directly or indirectly to my agent or his or her estate, or (iii) use my assets to discharge any of his or her legal obligations, including any obligation of support owed to others, excluding me and those I am legally obligated to support.

Your Agent May Make Gifts Only to Himself or Herself

Except as specified in this paragraph, my agent may not make gifts of my property or forgive debts owed to me. However, my agent may make gifts of my property to himself or herself as long as those gifts are not worth more than a total of $_____ in any calendar year.

Your Agent May Make Gifts to Anyone, Including Himself or Herself

My agent may make gifts of my property, including forgiveness of debts owed to me and completion of charitable pledges that I have made. However, my agent shall not make gifts of my property to himself or herself, or anyone he or she is legally obligated to support, worth more than a total of $_____ in any calendar year.

Your Agent May Make Gifts to Himself or Herself, and to Other People That You Name

My agent may make gifts of my property, including forgiveness of debts owed to me and completion of charitable pledges that I have made. However, the recipients of any such gifts shall be limited to _____*[insert the names of people to whom your agent may make gifts, joined with "or"]*_____. My agent may also make gifts of my property to himself or herself, provided that any gifts to my agent, or anyone he or she is legally obligated to support, are not worth more than a total of $_____ in any calendar year.

h. Creating, Modifying, Revoking, or Funding a Trust

Although your agent is not allowed to make, modify, or revoke a will for you, you may grant your agent the power to set up, modify, or terminate a trust on your behalf. Including this power in your document allows your agent to do some planning that will permit your estate to avoid probate or estate taxes. You need not worry that your agent will go against your wishes and alter a plan you've already created for distributing your property after death—for example,

by transferring assets you planned to leave by will into a new living trust and designating new beneficiaries for those assets. California law forbids an agent from changing your beneficiaries unless you specifically grant such authority in your power of attorney document. (Cal. Prob. Code § 4264; *Schubert v. Reynolds*, 95 Cal. App. 4th 100, 115 Cal. Rptr. 2d 285 (2002).)

If you want to grant your agent only the power to set up and manage a trust for you, but not to change who will inherit your property, here's a clause that you can use:

> My agent may create, modify, or revoke a trust on my behalf. If my agent creates a trust, my agent may designate or change trust beneficiaries but may not do so in a way that leaves property to different beneficiaries than those I have named in other estate planning documents.

On the other hand, if you want your agent to have the authority to change your beneficiaries, you can grant that broad power. If you want to give your agent this kind of control over your estate plan, it's very important that the two of you thoroughly discuss your wishes. And remember that your agent must always act in your best interests. Here is some language you can use to give broader powers to your agent:

> My agent may create, modify, or revoke a trust on my behalf. If my agent creates a trust, my agent may designate or change trust beneficiaries even if doing so leaves property to different beneficiaries than those I have named in other estate planning documents.

If you use one of the clauses above to allow your agent to set up a trust for you, you'll also want to give your agent the power to fund that trust by transferring property to it. (If you granted the estate and trusts power discussed in Section C4(H), above, your agent has the power to transfer items of your property into a revocable trust you've already created.) Here's the language to use:

My agent may fund with my property a trust created by me or created for my benefit by my agent.

Finally, be aware that if, in your durable power, you grant the power to modify or revoke a trust, the trust instrument itself must also permit it. If you have existing trusts over which you wish to give your agent control, you may have to modify the trust documents to ensure your agent will have the necessary power.

i.   Limits on the Agent's Authority

You can add your own restrictions or additions to the any of the powers you grant to your agent. For example, if a power listed on the form seems too broad, you can add limits to it. Here are a few examples:

(1) Restricting the Sale of Your Home
Selling your home, especially if you've lived there many years, can be a disturbing prospect. Some people feel quite strongly that the agent should not sell their home—no matter what happens. If you've granted the real estate power, but you want to forbid your agent from selling or mortgaging your home, you can include a provision like the one below.

> My agent shall have no authority to sell, convey, exchange, transfer, or partition the real property, or any rights or security interest therein, of my principal place of residence, located at _[insert the full address of your home]_ .

But think carefully before you tie the hands of your agent in this way. Of course you don't want to lose your home—but if a financial emergency makes it necessary, you may not want to leave your agent without options. Especially if your spouse or other co-owner of your home will be your agent, you probably want to trust that person to make a decision that's in your best interests.

(2) Restrictions on Running a Small Business
If you have given your agent power over your small business interests but want to restrict the agent's freedom to sell or encumber the business, you can include a clause like this one:

> My agent shall have no authority to sell, transfer, or otherwise encumber my business, _[type the name and address of your business]_ .

If you don't want to include an outright ban on selling the business, you may still want someone else—your spouse or financial advisor, perhaps—to review and approve a sale. If that's the case, include a clause like this:

> If my agent deems it necessary to sell _[specify the property]_ he or she shall do so only with the written approval of _[insert the name and address of the person who must approve]_ .

(3) Requiring the Approval of Others
You can require your agent to seek the approval of a trusted friend or family member before taking certain actions. If you wish to add this type of limitation to any power, you can use the following language:

> The agent's power to _[insert the power]_ may be exercised only upon written approval by _[insert the name and address of the person or people who must approve]_ .

j.   Making Periodic Reports

Unless you require it, your agent doesn't have to report to anyone about your finances. Usually, that's fine. In some circumstances, though, you may want to require reports. For example, you may be able to defuse a potentially explosive personal conflict by reassuring mistrustful family members that they'll receive regular reports about your finances. You can use a clause like this one to require periodic reports to people that you name:

My agent shall prepare written _[quarterly, semi-annual, annual, or whatever period you choose]_ reports regarding my finances, including the income received and expenses incurred by my agent for me during the previous _[insert correct number of months depending on the period you choose]_. These reports shall be mailed within 30 days of each _[quarter, six-month period, year, or whatever period you choose]_ to _[insert the names and addresses of people to whom your agent must make reports]_.

The idea of making your agent accountable to people may be appealing to you. But before you type up a long list of names of people to whom your agent must make reports, ask yourself whether these reports are truly necessary.

One of the most important reasons for making a power of attorney is to give control of your finances to someone you trust completely, bypassing the court system. One big advantage of this tactic is that you spare your agent the hassle and expense of preparing reports and accountings for a court.

If you want your agent to prepare reports so that someone can keep tabs on what he or she is doing, think again about the person you've named—and your level of trust.

k. Nominating a Conservator or Guardian

One last clause that you may want to include isn't really a special instruction to the agent, but it does concern the agent. It deals with what you want to happen in the highly unlikely event that a court proceeding is ever brought to set aside or override your durable power of attorney. (See Section A3.) If your durable power of attorney is declared invalid, the court will appoint a conservator to handle your financial affairs.

To guard against the possibility that your plans for financial management might be thwarted if a court appoints a conservator, you can provide, in your durable power of attorney, that you want the person you choose as agent to be named as the conservator. Even if it's not required by law, most courts will honor your request absent a powerful reason not to.

Here's a clause you can include in the special instructions section of your form to nominate your agent as conservator or guardian:

If, in a court proceeding, it is ever resolved that I need a conservator, guardian, or other person to administer and supervise my estate, I nominate my agent to serve in that capacity. If my agent cannot serve, I nominate my alternate agent to serve.

6. If You Appointed More Than One Agent

If you named more than one agent, look for the heading in the form titled "EXERCISE OF POWER OF ATTORNEY WHERE MORE THAN ONE AGENT DESIGNATED." (If you named only one agent, skip to the next step.) Here, you must state whether or not you want to allow each agent to act separately (independently) on your behalf or whether they must all agree before taking action. (See Section B4, above, for discussion of this issue.)

- To permit your agents to act independently, enter "separately" in the blank.
- To require your agents to act jointly, enter "jointly" in the blank.

7. Reliance by Third Parties

This clause tells a third party that it's safe to rely on the agent's authority when shown a copy of the durable power of attorney. (For a discussion of this issue, see Section A5, above.)

8. Signing Your Durable Power of Attorney

You must sign the power of attorney in the presence of a notary public. Instructions are in Section D, below.

9. Agent's Acceptance of Responsibility

This sentence at the end of the form means that if your agent exercises any authority under the power of attorney, he or she must act as your "fiduciary." A fiduciary must always act in your best interests. (For more information about your agent's legal responsibilities, see Section B3, above.)

D. Making Your Durable Power of Attorney Legal

After you've completed your durable power of attorney for finances, you must carry out a few simple tasks to make sure the document is legally valid. This section shows you what to do.

Making Your Document Legal

☐ Show the durable power of attorney to banks, brokers, insurers, and other financial institutions you expect your agent to deal with, to make sure they'll accept it.

☐ Sign the durable power of attorney in front of a notary public.

☐ Record (file) the durable power of attorney in the county land records office, if necessary.

☐ Distribute copies of the durable power of attorney to people the agent will deal with.

☐ Store the durable power of attorney where your agent will have quick access to it.

---

1. Before You Sign

Before you finalize your power of attorney, you may want to show it to the banks, brokers, insurers, and other financial institutions you expect your agent to deal with on your behalf.

Discussing your plans with people at these institutions now (and giving them a copy of the durable power of attorney, after you sign it, if you wish),

can make your agent's job easier. An institution may ask that you use its own form or include specific language in your durable power of attorney, authorizing the agent to do certain things on your behalf. You may have to go along if you want cooperation later.

2. Sign and Notarize the Durable Power of Attorney

A durable power of attorney is a serious document, and to make it effective you must observe certain formalities when you sign it. Fortunately, these requirements aren't difficult to meet.

You must sign your durable power of attorney in the presence of a notary public for the state of California. California law requires this. (Cal. Prob. Code § 4402(c).)

The notary public watches you sign the durable power of attorney and then signs it too and stamps it with an official seal. The notary will want proof of your identity, such as a driver's license that bears your photo and signature. The notary's fee is usually just a few dollars—about $10 in most places.

Finding a notary public shouldn't be a problem; many advertise in the Yellow Pages. Or check with your bank, which may provide notarizations as a service to customers. Real estate offices and title companies also have notaries.

If you are gravely ill, you'll need to find a notary who will come to your home or hospital room. To arrange it, call around to notaries listed in the Yellow Pages. Expect to pay a reasonable extra fee for a house call.

3. Putting Your Durable Power of Attorney on Public Record

You may need to put a copy of your durable power of attorney on file in the county recorder's office of any counties where you own real estate. The process of filing your document is called "recording."

Sample Durable Power of Attorney for Finances

Uniform Statutory Form Power of Attorney
California Probate Code Section 4402

NOTICE: THE POWERS GRANTED BY THIS DOCUMENT ARE BROAD AND SWEEPING. THEY ARE EXPLAINED IN THE UNIFORM STATUTORY FORM POWER OF ATTORNEY ACT (CALIFORNIA PROBATE CODE SECTIONS 4400-4465). IF YOU HAVE ANY QUESTIONS ABOUT THESE POWERS, OBTAIN COMPETENT LEGAL ADVICE. THIS DOCUMENT DOES NOT AUTHORIZE ANYONE TO MAKE MEDICAL AND OTHER HEALTH CARE DECISIONS FOR YOU. YOU MAY REVOKE THIS POWER OF ATTORNEY IF YOU LATER WISH TO DO SO.

I <u>Lillian L. Woo, 8892 Grant St., Sacramento, CA 95822</u> ,
Your Name and Address

appoint <u>Robert M. Woo, 8892 Grant St., Sacramento, CA 95822</u> ,
Name and Address of the Person Appointed, or of Each Person Appointed If You Want to Designate More Than One

as my agent (attorney-in-fact) to act for me in any lawful way with respect to the following initialed subjects:

TO GRANT ALL OF THE FOLLOWING POWERS, INITIAL THE LINE IN FRONT OF (N) AND IGNORE THE LINES IN FRONT OF THE OTHER POWERS.

TO GRANT ONE OR MORE, BUT FEWER THAN ALL OF THE FOLLOWING POWERS, INITIAL THE LINE IN FRONT OF EACH POWER YOU ARE GRANTING.

TO WITHHOLD A POWER, DO NOT INITIAL THE LINE IN FRONT OF IT. YOU MAY, BUT NEED NOT, CROSS OUT EACH POWER WITHHELD.

INITIALS

_____ (A) Real property transactions.

_____ (B) Tangible personal property transactions.

_____ (C) Stock and bond transactions.

_____ (D) Commodity and option transactions.

_____ (E) Banking and other financial institution transactions.

_____ (F) Business operating transactions.

_____ (G) Insurance and annuity transactions.

_____ (H) Estate, trust, and other beneficiary transactions.

_____ (I) Claims and litigation.

_____ (J) Personal and family maintenance.

_____ (K) Benefits from Social Security, Medicare, Medicaid, or other governmental programs, or civil or military service.

_____ (L) Retirement plan transactions.

_____ (M) Tax matters.

*LLW* (N) ALL OF THE POWERS LISTED ABOVE.

YOU NEED NOT INITIAL ANY OTHER LINES IF YOU INITIAL LINE (N).

Sample Durable Power of Attorney for Finances (continued)

Special Instructions

ON THE FOLLOWING LINES YOU MAY GIVE SPECIAL INSTRUCTION LIMITING OR EXTENDING THE POWERS GRANTED TO YOUR AGENT.

If Robert M. Woo does not or ceases to serve as agent, I appoint Elaine P. Woo, 834 D St., Sacramento, CA, 95822 to serve as agent

My agent may buy any assets of mine or engage in any transaction he or she deems in good faith to be in my interest, no matter what the interest or benefit to my agent.

My agent may commingle any of my funds with his or hers. However, if an alternate agent is serving under the document the alternate may not commingle any of my funds with his or hers.

My agent may delegate, in writing, any authority granted under this power of attorney to a person he or she selects. Any such delegation shall state the period during which it's valid and specify the extent of the delegation.

UNLESS YOU DIRECT OTHERWISE ABOVE, THIS POWER OF ATTORNEY IS EFFECTIVE IMMEDIATELY AND WILL CONTINUE UNTIL IT IS REVOKED.

This power of attorney will continue to be effective even though I become incapacitated.

STRIKE THE PRECEDING SENTENCE IF YOU DO NOT WANT THIS POWER OF ATTORNEY TO CONTINUE IF YOU BECOME INCAPACITATED.

EXERCISE OF POWER OF ATTORNEY WHERE MORE THAN ONE AGENT DESIGNATED:

If I have designated more than one agent, the agents are to act _____.

IF YOU APPOINTED MORE THAN ONE AGENT AND YOU WANT EACH AGENT TO BE ABLE TO ACT ALONE WITHOUT THE OTHER AGENT JOINING, WRITE THE WORD "SEPARATELY" IN THE BLANK SPACE ABOVE. IF YOU DO NOT INSERT ANY WORD IN THE BLANK SPACE, OR IF YOU INSERT THE WORD "JOINTLY," THEN ALL OF YOUR AGENTS MUST ACT OR SIGN TOGETHER.

I agree that any third party who receives a copy of this document may act under it. Revocation of the power of attorney is not effective as to a third party until the third party has actual knowledge of the revocation. I

Sample Durable Power of Attorney for Finances (continued)

agree to indemnify the third party for any claims that arise against the third party because of reliance on this power of attorney.

Signed this _____16th_____ day of _____September_____, 20 _04_

Lillian L. Woo
Your Signature

_343-54-1291_
Your Social Security Number

State of California, County of _____Sacramento_____

BY ACCEPTING OR ACTING UNDER THE APPOINTMENT, THE AGENT ASSUMES THE FIDUCIARY AND OTHER LEGAL RESPONSIBILITIES OF AN AGENT.

Certificate of Acknowledgment of Notary Public

State of California

County of _____Sacramento_____ } ss

On _____September 16_____, _2004_, before me, _____Rose Livingston_____,
personally appeared _____Lillian L. Woo_____,
personally known to me (or proved on the basis of satisfactory evidence) to be the person whose name is subscribed to the within instrument, and acknowledged to me that he or she executed the same in his or her authorized capacity and that by his or her signature on the instrument, the person, or the entity upon behalf of which the person acted, executed the instrument.

WITNESS my hand and official seal.

Rose Livingston

Notary Public for the State of California

[NOTARY SEAL]   My commission expires _____June 12, 2007_____

a. When You Should Record Your Durable Power of Attorney

You must record the power of attorney only if it gives your agent authority over your real estate. Essentially, this means you must record the document if you granted the real estate power. In this case, if the document isn't in the public records, your agent won't be able to sell, mortgage, or transfer your real estate.

Recording makes it clear to all interested parties that the agent has power over the property. County land records are checked whenever real estate changes hands or is mortgaged; if your agent goes to sell or mortgage your real estate, there must be something in these public records that proves he or she has authority to do so.

There is no time limit on when you must record a durable power of attorney. If you don't expect your agent to act for you for many years (or ever), you may not want to record it immediately. Your agent can always record it later, if the document takes effect.

Even if recording is not legally required, you can go ahead and record your durable power of attorney; officials in some financial institutions may be reassured later on by seeing that you took that step.

b. Where to Record Your Power of Attorney

In California, each county has its own county recorder's office. Take the durable power of attorney to the local office in the county where your real estate is located. If you want your agent to have authority over real estate in more than one county, record the power of attorney in each county where you own property.

c. How to Record a Document

Recording a document is easy. You may even be able to do it by mail, but it's safer to go in person. The clerk will make a copy (usually on microfilm

these days) for the public record. It will be assigned a reference number, often in terms of books and pages—for example, "Book 14, Page 1932, of the Contra Costa County, California, records." In most places, it costs just a few dollars per page to record a document. If you have questions or need more information, call the county recorder's office; you can find the number in the Government Listings section of the white pages under "Recorder" or "County Recorder."

4. What to Do With the Signed Document

The agent will need the original document to carry out your wishes.

If the power of attorney is to take effect immediately, give the original, signed and notarized document to the agent. If you named more than one agent, give the original document to one of them. Between them, they will have to work out the best way to prove their authority. For example, they may decide to visit some financial institutions or government offices together to establish themselves as your agents. Or they may need to take turns with the document. Some agencies, such as the IRS, will accept a copy of the document, rather than the original.

If the durable power of attorney won't become effective unless you become incapacitated (a springing durable power of attorney), keep the notarized, signed original yourself. Store it in a safe, convenient place to which the agent has quick access. A fireproof box in your home or office is fine. Just make sure the agent knows where it is.

A safe deposit box isn't the best place to store a springing durable power of attorney, unless the agent is a cotenant with access to the box. It's true that the power of attorney may give your agent the authority to open your safe deposit box, but if the document is locked in the box to begin with, the bank won't be able to confirm your agent's authority and your agent will be stuck. It's better just to keep the document wherever you file other important legal papers.

5. Making and Distributing Copies

If you wish, you can give copies of your durable power to the people your agent will need to deal with—banks or government offices, for example. If the durable power is already in their records, it may eliminate hassles for your agent later.

If you're making a springing durable power of attorney, however, it may seem premature to contact people and institutions about a document that may never go into effect. It's up to you.

Be sure to keep a list of everyone to whom you give a copy. If you later revoke your durable power of attorney, you must notify each institution of the revocation. (See Section E, below.)

6. Keeping Your Document Up to Date

If you make a springing durable power of attorney, it's a good idea to revoke it and create a new one every five to seven years, especially if your circumstances have changed significantly. A durable power of attorney never expires, but if the document was signed many years before it goes into effect, the agent may have more difficulty getting banks, insurance companies, or people in government agencies to accept its authority.

E. Revoking a Durable Power of Attorney for Finances

After you make a power of attorney for finances, you can revoke it at any time, as long as you are of sound mind. Just carefully follow the procedure set out in this section.

Revoking a Durable Power of Attorney for Finances

☐ Prepare a Notice of Revocation.
☐ Sign the Notice of Revocation in front of a notary public.
☐ Record the Notice of Revocation at the county recorder's office, if necessary.
☐ Deliver a copy of the Notice of Revocation to the agent and each institution and person who has dealt or might deal with the former agent.

a. When to Revoke a Durable Power of Attorney for Finances

Here are the most common situations in which you should revoke a power of attorney and start fresh.

You want to change the terms of the power of attorney. There is no accepted way to amend a power of attorney. If you want to change your document—for example, to change the powers or to name a different agent—the safe course is to revoke the existing document and prepare a new one. Don't go back and modify your old document with pen, typewriter, or correction fluid—you could throw doubt on the authenticity of the whole thing.

If your agent won't let go. An agent who refuses to accept a revocation can create serious problems. If you get into a dispute with your agent over whether or not your revocation is valid, consult a lawyer.

You move to another state. If you move to a new state, your agent may run into some trouble getting others to accept the validity of a power of attorney document signed in your former state. It's best to revoke your power of attorney and prepare a new document.

You lose the power of attorney document. If you conclude that you've really lost your signed power of attorney document, it's wise to formally revoke it, destroy any copies, and create a new one. Very few people are likely to accept your agent's authority if they can't look at the original document it's based on. By officially revoking the lost version, you minimize chances that it will cause confusion if it reappears someday.

You get married or divorced. If you get married after signing a power of attorney, you'll probably want to designate your new spouse to be your agent, if you named someone else originally.

As mentioned earlier (see Section A3), if you name your spouse as your agent and later divorce, you should revoke the power of attorney and create a new one, naming someone else as your agent. It's wise for separating domestic partners to do this, too.

Your agent becomes unavailable. If the person you named as your agent moves away, becomes ill, or is no longer closely involved with your life, you should appoint someone else to serve. To do that, revoke the old power of attorney and prepare a new one.

Your durable power is old. As discussed in Section D6, if you make a springing durable power of attorney, it's a good idea to review it every five to seven years. If the document is signed many years before it goes into effect, the agent may have trouble getting others to accept it. You may want to revoke the document and make a new one.

b. How to Revoke a Durable Power of Attorney for Finances

Practically speaking, there are two ways to revoke your power of attorney for finances:

- By preparing and signing a document called a Notice of Revocation
- By telling your agent that his or her authority is revoked and destroying all copies of the power of attorney document.

The first method is preferable, because it creates proof that you really revoked the power of attorney. Here's how to proceed.

(1) Prepare a Notice of Revocation

The purpose of a Notice of Revocation is to notify your agent, and those he or she may have been dealing with, that you have revoked the durable power of attorney.

This book contains two kinds of Notice of Revocation forms for you to use. If you didn't record your power of attorney in the county land records office, use the standard form. If you did record the original power of attorney, you must also record the revocation; use the Notice of Revocation for a recorded power of attorney. Sample forms follow; you can find the blank forms in Appendix B and on the enclosed CD-ROM.

(2) Sign and Notarize the Revocation

You must sign and date the Notice of Revocation in front of a notary public. For information about finding a notary and getting your signature notarized, see Section D2, above.

(3) Record the Notice of Revocation

If you recorded the original power of attorney at the county recorder's office, you must also record the revocation. How to record a document is explained in Section D3, above.

But even if the original power of attorney was not recorded, you can record a revocation if you fear that the former agent might try to act without authorization. If the revocation is part of the public record, people who check those records (as anyone should if real estate is involved) will know that the former agent is no longer authorized to act on your behalf.

(4) Notify Anyone Who Deals With the Former Agent

It's not enough to sign a revocation, or even to record it, for it to be properly effective; there's one more crucial step. You must send a copy of the Notice of Revocation to the former agent and all institutions and people who have dealt or might deal with the former agent.

If you don't give this written notification, people or institutions who don't know the power of attorney has been revoked might still enter into transactions with the former agent. If they do this in good faith, they are legally protected. (Cal. Prob. Code § 4151(b).) You could be held legally liable for the acts of your

Sample Notice of Revocation of Power of Attorney: Unrecorded

Notice of Revocation of Power of Attorney

I, _Ramona Ellsworth_ ,

of the City of _Hornbrook_ , County of _Siskiyou_ ,

State of California, revoke the power of attorney dated _September 15, 1999_ , empowering

Bill Piersall

to act as my agent. I revoke and withdraw all power and authority granted under that power of attorney.

Dated: _February 5, 2004_

Ramona Ellsworth
Signature of Principal

Ramona Ellsworth , Principal

Certificate of Acknowlegment of Notary Public

State of California

County of _Siskiyou_ } ss

On _February 5_ , _2004_ , before me, _Daniel Sweeny_ ,

personally appeared _Ramona Ellsworth_ ,

personally known to me (or proved on the basis of satisfactory evidence) to be the person whose name is subscribed to the within instrument, and acknowledged to me that he or she executed the same in his or her authorized capacity and that by his or her signature on the instrument, the person, or the entity upon behalf of which the person acted, executed the instrument.

WITNESS my hand and official seal.

Daniel Sweeny

Notary Public for the State of California

[NOTARY SEAL]   My commission expires _April 1, 2008_

Sample Notice of Revocation of Power of Attorney: Recorded

RECORDING REQUESTED BY

AND WHEN RECORDED MAIL TO

David L. Hernandez

45 N. Palm Drive

Blythe, CA 92225

Notice of Revocation of Power of Attorney

I, __David L. Hernandez__ ,

of the City of __Bythe__ , County of __Riverside__ ,

State of California, revoke the power of attorney dated __May 26, 2000__ , empowering

__Francis M. Rowland__

to act as my agent. I revoke and withdraw all power and authority granted under that power of attorney.

That power of attorney was recorded on __May 30__ , __2000__ , in Book

__421__ , at Page __2436__ of the Official Records, County of __Riverside__ ,

State of California.

Dated: __November 2, 2004__

__David L. Hernandez__
Signature of Principal

__David L. Hernandez__ , Principal

Certificate of Acknowlegment of Notary Public

State of California

County of __Riverside__ } ss

On __November 3__ , __2004__ , before me, __Evelyn Kramer__ ,

personally appeared __David L. Hernandez__ ,

personally known to me (or proved on the basis of satisfactory evidence) to be the person whose name is subscribed to the within instrument, and acknowledged to me that he or she executed the same in his or her authorized capacity and that by his or her signature on the instrument, the person, or the entity upon behalf of which the person acted, executed the instrument.

WITNESS my hand and official seal.

__Evelyn Kramer__

Notary Public for the State of California

[NOTARY SEAL]   My commission expires __August 1, 2007__

agent, even though you have revoked his or her authority. In other words, the legal burden is on you to be sure everyone knows you have revoked the power of attorney.

When you're ready to send out revocation notices, try to think of everyone with whom the agent may have had dealings. Here are some examples:

- banks
- mortgage companies
- title companies
- stockbrokers
- insurance companies
- credit card companies
- Social Security offices
- Medicare or Medicaid offices
- IRS
- pension fund administrators
- post offices
- hospitals
- doctors
- schools
- relatives
- business partners
- landlords
- lawyers
- accountants
- real estate agents
- maintenance and repair people.

■

5

Help Beyond the Book

When you prepare your own advance health care directive and durable power of attorney for finances with this book, you probably won't need to see a lawyer. If, however, you have specific questions or unusual circumstances —for example, the potential for family squabbles, worries about your agent's powers, or a very large amount of property—you may want or need legal advice.

If you do need more legal information or advice, you can talk to a lawyer or look for the answers yourself, by going to the law library or by searching for information online. (Many people do a little of both.) If you just want clerical help typing or recording your document, you may want to get help from a document preparer.

A. Document Preparers

Even if you need "legal" help, you may not need a lawyer. People who operate document preparation services, also known as independent paralegals, are experts at typing up legal documents. They are not lawyers and do not give legal advice, but if you know what you want, a document preparer can help you prepare the legal paperwork at an affordable price. For example, if you need to retype one of the forms in this book—say you need more room for special instructions in your durable power of attorney for finances or you want to remove optional parts of your advance health care directive—and you're concerned about getting everything in the right place, a document preparer can probably help.

Here are some things to look for when choosing a document preparer:

An established or recommended service. Few document preparers stay in business unless they provide honest and competent services. A recommendation from a social service agency, friend, court clerk, or lawyer is probably a good place to take your business.

Reasonable fees. California document preparers will probably charge between $50 and $125 to type up your documents, depending on where you live and the complexity of your forms.

Trained staff. One indication of whether or not people are committed to providing good services is if they have undertaken skills training through independent paralegal associations and continuing education seminars.

B. Lawyers

Lawyers are costly. Estate planning fees usually range from $150 to $400 per hour. But if your situation is complex and you want professional help, a good estate planning specialist can be well worth the cost.

1. Looking for a Lawyer

Ideally, you'll find an attorney with whom you have personal rapport and who treats you as an equal. Here are some suggestions to help you find a lawyer you'll like.

Ask your family, friends, and acquaintances. When looking for a good lawyer, especially an estate planning expert, personal contacts are the traditional, and probably the best, method. If a relative or friend who has good business and financial sense recommends an estate planning lawyer, chances are you'll like the lawyer, too. If nothing turns up, check with people you know in any business, political, or social organization with which you're involved, especially those with a large number of members over age 40. Assuming they themselves have good sense, they may well be able to point you to a competent lawyer who handles estate planning matters and whose point of view is similar to yours.

Ask another lawyer. Another good approach is to ask for help from a lawyer you know and like personally, but who works in another legal field. Very likely the lawyer you know can refer you to a trustworthy estate planning expert.

Ask small business owners. Yet another possibility is to check with people you respect who own their own small businesses. Almost anyone running a small business has a relationship with a lawyer, and chances are they've found one they like. Again, this lawyer will probably not be an estate planning expert, but will likely know one—or several.

⚠️ **Beware of legal referral services.** A lawyer referral service will usually be able to give you the names of some attorneys who practice in your geographic area. Most county bar associations have referral services, and these days you can find referral services of all kinds online. But referral services usually provide only minimal screening for the attorneys they list, which means that those who participate may not be the most experienced or competent. It may be possible to find a skilled attorney through a referral service, but be sure to ask the attorney about credentials and experience.

2. Working With a Lawyer

Before you talk to a lawyer, try to decide what kind of help you really need. Do you want someone to review your documents to make sure they look all right? Or do you want advice on a complete estate plan? If you don't clearly tell the lawyer what you want, you may find yourself agreeing to more than you'd planned.

Before you see a lawyer, a good strategy is to write down your questions as specifically as you can. If the lawyer doesn't give you clear, concise answers, say thank you and try someone else. Preparing a valid durable power of attorney for finances and health care directive isn't an overly complicated job in most cases; a knowledgeable lawyer should be able to give you satisfactory answers on the spot.

If the lawyer acts wise but says little except to ask that matters be placed in his or her hands—for a substantial fee, of course—watch out. You're either dealing with someone who doesn't know the answer and won't admit it or someone who finds it impossible to let go of the idea that, as an expert, he or she doesn't have a responsibility to treat you as an equal. Both of these things are all too common, and you deserve better.

3. Lawyer's Fees

Fees for estate planning lawyers can be steep—sometimes hundreds of dollars an hour. But price is not always related to quality. A fancy office, corporate clothes, and a solemn face are no guarantee (or even a reasonable indication) that a lawyer is competent, but these things usually do guarantee a high price tag. Fortunately, many good lawyers operate more modestly and pass the savings on to their clients.

No matter how much you like your lawyer, be sure to settle your fee arrangement—in writing—at the start of your relationship. In addition to the amount charged per hour, it's also prudent to get an estimate of how many hours your lawyer expects to spend on the work.

C. Getting More Information on Your Own

As you prepare your documents, you may find yourself wanting to know more about a particular aspect of the law. For instance, you may want to look up some of the California Probate Code sections that are listed in this book, to learn more details about a particular matter or just to read the law itself.

Fortunately, the laws governing medical directives and powers of attorney are not particularly difficult to research. But first, you'll need to find a law library or a computer with Internet access.

1. Going to a Law Library

There are several kinds of law libraries available to you:

- a public law library (usually located in or near the county courthouse)
- a public library with a good law collection, or
- a library at a public (or even private, if you ask permission) law school.

When you get to the library, you'll need the help of a kind reference librarian to point you in the right direction. Thankfully, law librarians are almost always helpful and courteous to nonlawyers who undertake their own legal research.

The California Probate Code. The first thing to do is ask the librarian where to find the California Probate Code. This is where you're going to find most of the laws that govern estate planning and planning for incapacity in California. If you can, get an "annotated version," which contains both the state statutes and excerpts from any relevant court cases and refererences to related articles.

Once you've found the probate code, you can look up the laws that govern medical directives and powers of attorney. The laws you want will be grouped together in a few different areas of the code. You'll probably be most interested in Sections 4000 to 4545, which govern powers of attorney for finances, and Sections 4600 to 4948, governing health care matters.

California Laws	
Here's where to turn in the California Probate Code to find some of the laws you may need:	
Advance Health Care Directives	Sections 4600-4948
DNR Orders	Sections 4780-4786
Durable Powers of Attorney for Finances	Sections 4000-4545
Conservatorship Proceedings	Sections 1800-2955

When you find what you're looking for, make sure you're reading the most recent version of the statute by checking the back of the statute book to see if there's a supplement (called a "pocket part") inserted inside the back cover. Pocket parts contain statutory changes (and summaries of related court decisions) made since the hardback book was printed.

Be warned that statutes are rarely easy to read. Commonly, they are written in dense prose, full of incredibly long sentences, obscure legal terms, and cross-references to other statutes. Wade through them as best you can, and expect to read any section you're interested in several times. Take comfort—most lawyers have to do the same.

After you've looked at the basic law, you'll probably want to check any recent court decisions mentioned in the "Annotation" section of the code that immediately follows the law itself.

Form books. Form books, which are how-to-do-it books written primarily for lawyers, can also be helpful. In particular, you should ask the law librarian to point you to *California Durable Powers of Attorney* from Continuing Education of the Bar (CEB), which is a very comprehensive and not-too-convoluted lawyer's guide to helping clients plan for incapacity. This form book comes in a big binder, and it delves more deeply into some of the issues we've discussed in earlier chapters, including drafting specific clauses for complicated health care or financial situations, and determining mental capacity.

2. Online Legal Research

Another, usually quicker way to find the information you need is to use your computer. You can look up any section of the California Probate Code online by visiting Nolo's legal research center at www.nolo .com/research/index.html. Once there, follow these steps to look up the law you need:

1. Click "State Laws."
2. Choose "California."
3. Check the "Probate Code" box.
4. Enter the number of the section you want to see (this will probably be a specific section mentioned somewhere in this book or the sections mentioned above).

It's that easy. You can also browse Nolo's website for lots of other helpful legal information and links. The best place to start is the free legal encyclopedia, which contains dozens of articles on estate planning.

More help finding the law. *Legal Research: How to Find & Understand the Law,* by Stephen Elias and Susan Levinkind (Nolo), is a hands-on guide to research on the Internet and in the law library. It addresses research methods in detail and should answer most questions that arise in the course of your research. In particular, it contains a good discussion of how to read and analyze statutes, and instructions for looking up legal cases. ■

How to Use the CD-ROM

The tear-out forms in Appendix B are included on a CD-ROM in the back of the book. This CD-ROM, which can be used with Windows computers, installs files that can be opened, printed, and edited using a word processor or other software. It is *not* a stand-alone software program. Please read this Appendix and the README.TXT file included on the CD-ROM for instructions on using the Forms CD.

Note to Mac users: This CD-ROM and its files should also work on Macintosh computers. Please note, however, that Nolo cannot provide technical support for non-Windows users.

How to View the README File

If you do not know how to view the file README.TXT, insert the Forms CD-ROM into your computer's CD-ROM drive and follow these instructions:

- Windows 9x, 2000, Me and XP: (1) On your PC's desktop, double-click the My Computer icon; (2) double-click the icon for the CD-ROM drive into which the Forms CD-ROM was inserted; (3) double-click the file README.TXT.
- Macintosh: (1) On your Mac desktop, double-click the icon for the CD-ROM that you inserted; (2) double-click on the file README.TXT.

While the README file is open, print it out by using the Print command in the File menu.

Two different kinds of forms are contained on the CD-ROM:

- Word processing (RTF) forms that you can open, complete, print and save with your word processing program (see Section B, below), and

- Forms (PDF) that can be viewed only with Adobe Acrobat Reader 4.0 or higher. You can install Acrobat Reader from the Forms CD (see Section C, below). These forms are designed to be printed out and filled in by hand or with a typewriter.

See Appendix B for a list of forms, their file names and file formats.

A. Installing the Form Files Onto Your Computer

Before you can do anything with the files on the CD-ROM, you need to install them onto your hard disk. In accordance with U.S. copyright laws, remember that copies of the CD-ROM and its files are for your personal use only.

Insert the Forms CD and do the following:

1. Windows 9x, 2000, Me and XP Users

Follow the instructions that appear on the screen. (If nothing happens when you insert the Forms CD-ROM, then (1) double-click the My Computer icon; (2) double-click the icon for the CD-ROM drive into which the Forms CD-ROM was inserted; and (3) double-click the file WELCOME.EXE.)

By default, all the files are installed to the \CA Power of Attorney Forms folder in the \Program Files folder of your computer. A folder called "CA Power of Attorney Forms" is added to the "Programs" folder of the Start menu.

2. Macintosh Users

Step 1: If the "CA Power of Attorney CD" window is not open, open it by double-clicking the "CA Power of Attorney CD" icon.

Step 2: Select the "CA Power of Attorney Forms" folder icon.

Step 3: Drag and drop the folder icon onto the icon of your hard disk.

B. Using the Word Processing Files to Create Documents

This section concerns the files for forms that can be opened and edited with your word processing program.

All word processing forms come in rich text format. These files have the extension ".RTF." For example, the form for the Advance Health Care Directive discussed in Chapter 2 is on the file HealthCareDir.RTF. All forms, their file names and file formats are listed in Appendix B.

RTF files can be read by most recent word processing programs, including all versions of MS Word for Windows and Macintosh, WordPad for Windows, and recent versions of WordPerfect for Windows and Macintosh.

To use a form from the CD to create your documents you must: (1) open a file in your word processor or text editor; (2) edit the form by filling in the required information; (3) print it out; (4) rename and save your revised file.

The following are general instructions on how to do this. However, each word processor uses different commands to open, format, save, and print documents. Please read your word processor's manual for specific instructions on performing these tasks.

Do not call Nolo's technical support if you have questions on how to use your word processor.

Step 1: Opening a File

There are three ways to open the word processing files included on the CD-ROM after you have installed them onto your computer.

- Windows users can open a file by selecting its "shortcut" as follows: (1) Click the Windows "Start" button; (2) open the "Programs" folder; (3) open the "CA Power of Attorney Forms" subfolder; and (4) click on the shortcut to the form you want to work with.
- Both Windows and Macintosh users can open a file directly by double clicking on it. Use My Computer or Windows Explorer (Windows 9x, 2000, Me or XP) or the Finder (Macintosh) to go to the folder you installed or copied the CD-ROM's files to. Then, double-click on the specific file you want to open.
- You can also open a file from within your word processor. To do this, you must first start your word processor. Then, go to the File menu and choose the Open command. This opens a dialog box where you will tell the program (1) the type of file you want to open (*.RTF); and (2) the location and name of the file (you will need to navigate through the directory tree to get to the folder on your hard disk where the CD's files have been installed). If these directions are unclear, you will need to look through the manual for your word processing program—Nolo's technical support department will *not* be able to help you with the use of your word processing program.

Where Are the Files Installed?

Windows Users
RTF files are installed by default to a folder named \CA Power of Attorney Forms in the \Program Files folder of your computer.

Macintosh Users
RTF files are located in the "CA Power of Attorney Forms" folder.

Step 2: Editing Your Document

Fill in the appropriate information according to the instructions and sample agreements in the book. Underlines are used to indicate where you need to enter your information, frequently followed by instructions in brackets. *Be sure to delete the underlines and instructions from your edited document.* If you do not know how to use your word processor to edit a document, you will need to look through the manual for your word processing program—Nolo's technical support department will *not* be able to help you with the use of your word processing program.

Editing Forms That Have Optional or Alternative Text

Some of the forms have check boxes before text. The check boxes indicate:

- Optional text, where you choose whether to include or exclude the given text.
- Alternative text, where you select one alternative to include and exclude the other alternatives.

If you are using the tear-out forms in Appendix B, you simply mark the appropriate box to make your choice.

If you are using the Forms CD, however, we recommend that instead of marking the check boxes, you do the following:

Optional text

If you don't want to include optional text, just delete it from your document.

If you do want to include optional text, just leave it in your document.

In either case, delete the check box itself as well as the italicized instructions that the text is optional.

Alternative text

First delete all the alternatives that you do not want to include.

Then delete the remaining check boxes, as well as the italicized instructions that you need to select one of the alternatives provided.

Step 3: Printing Out the Document

Use your word processor's or text editor's "Print" command to print out your document. If you do not know how to use your word processor to print a document, you will need to look through the manual for your word processing program—Nolo's technical support department will *not* be able to help you with the use of your word processing program.

Step 4: Saving Your Document

After filling in the form, use the "Save As" command to save and rename the file. Because all the files are "read-only," you will not be able to use the "Save" command. This is for your protection. *If you save the file without renaming it, the underlines that indicate where you need to enter your information will be lost and you will not be able to create a new document with this file without recopying the original file from the CD-ROM.*

If you do not know how to use your word processor to save a document, you will need to look through the manual for your word processing program—Nolo's technical support department will *not* be able to help you with the use of your word processing program.

C. Using PDF Files to Print Out Forms

An electronic copy of a Wallet Medical Emergency Card is included on the CD-ROM in Adobe Acrobat PDF format. You must have the Adobe Acrobat Reader installed on your computer (see below) to use this file. All forms, their file names and file formats, are listed in Appendix B.

This card cannot be filled out using your computer. To complete your card using this file, you must: (1) open the file; (2) print it out; and (3) complete it by hand or typewriter.

Installing Acrobat Reader

To install the Adobe Acrobat Reader, insert the CD into your computer's CD-ROM drive and follow these instructions:

- Windows 9x, 2000, Me and XP: Follow the instructions that appear on screen. (If nothing happens when you insert the Forms CD-ROM, then (1) double-click the My Computer icon; (2) double-click the icon for the CD-ROM drive into which the Forms CD-ROM was inserted; and (3) double-click the file WELCOME.EXE.)
- Macintosh: (1) If the "CA Power of Attorney CD" window is not open, open it by double-clicking the "CA Power of Attorney CD" icon; and (2) double-click on the "Acrobat Reader Installer" icon.

If you do not know how to use Adobe Acrobat to view and print the files, you will need to consult the online documentation that comes with the Acrobat Reader program.

Do *not* call Nolo technical support if you have questions on how to use Acrobat Reader.

go to the folder you created and copied the CD-ROM's files to. Then, double-click on the specific file you want to open.

- You can also open a PDF file from within Acrobat Reader. To do this, you must first start Reader. Then, go to the File menu and choose the Open command. This opens a dialog box where you will tell the program the location and name of the file (you will need to navigate through the directory tree to get to the folder on your hard disk where the CD's files have been installed). If these directions are unclear, you will need to look through Acrobat Reader's help—Nolo's technical support department will *not* be able to help you with the use of Acrobat Reader.

Where Are the PDF Files Installed?

Windows Users
PDF files are installed by default to a folder named \CA Power of Attorney Forms in the \Program Files folder of your computer.

Macintosh Users
PDF files are located in the "CA Power of Attorney Forms" folder.

Step 1: Opening PDF Files

PDF files, like the word processing files, can be opened one of three ways.

- Windows users can open a file by selecting its "shortcut" as follows: (1) Click the Windows "Start" button; (2) open the "Programs" folder; (3) open the "CA Power of Attorney Forms" subfolder; and (4) click on the shortcut to the form you want to work with.
- Both Windows and Macintosh users can open a file directly by double-clicking on it. Use My Computer or Windows Explorer (Windows 9x, 2000, Me or XP) or the Finder (Macintosh) to

Step 2: Printing PDF files

Choose Print from the Acrobat Reader File menu. This will open the Print dialog box. In the "Print Range" section of the Print dialog box, select the appropriate print range, then click OK.

Step 3: Filling in PDF files

PDF files cannot be filled out using your computer. To create your document using a PDF file, you must first print it out (see Step 2, above), and then complete it by hand or typewriter. ■

Tear-Out Forms

Name of Form	CD-ROM File Name	Chapter in Book
Advance Health Care Directive	HealthCareDir.RTF	2
Wallet Medical Emergency Card	WalletCard.PDF	2
Revocation of Advance Health Care Directive	HealthDirRevoc.RTF	2
Do Not Resuscitate (DNR) Order	NoResuscitate.RTF	3
Uniform Statutory Form Power of Attorney	PowAttorney.RTF	4
Physician's Determination of Incapacity	Incapacity.RTF	4
Revocation of Durable Power of Attorney for Finances: Recorded	RecPowRevoc.RTF	4
Revocation of Durable Power of Attorney for Finances: Unrecorded	UnrecPowRevoc.RTF	4

Advance Health Care Directive

Explanation

You have the right to give instructions about your own health care. You also have the right to name someone else to make health care decisions for you. This form lets you do either or both of these things. It also lets you express your wishes regarding donation of organs and the designation of your primary physician. If you use this form, you may complete or modify all or any part of it. You are free to use a different form.

Part 1 of this form is a power of attorney for health care. Part 1 lets you name another individual as agent to make health care decisions for you if you become incapable of making your own decisions or if you want someone else to make those decisions for you now even though you are still capable. You may also name an alternate agent to act for you if your first choice is not willing, able, or reasonably available to make decisions for you. (Your agent may not be an operator or employee of a community care facility or a residential care facility where you are receiving care, or your supervising health care provider or employee of the health care institution where you are receiving care, unless your agent is related to you, is your registered domestic partner, or is a coworker.)

Unless the form you sign limits the authority of your agent, your agent may make all health care decisions for you. This form has a place for you to limit the authority of your agent. You need not limit the authority of your agent if you wish to rely on your agent for all health care decisions that may have to be made. If you choose not to limit the authority of your agent, your agent will have the right to:

- Consent or refuse consent to any care, treatment, service, or procedure to maintain, diagnose, or otherwise affect a physical or mental condition.
- Select or discharge health care providers and institutions.

- Approve or disapprove diagnostic tests, surgical procedures, and programs of medication.
- Direct the provision, withholding, or withdrawal of artificial nutrition and hydration and all other forms of health care, including cardiopulmonary resuscitation.
- Make anatomical gifts, authorize an autopsy, and direct disposition of remains.

Part 2 of this form lets you give specific instructions about any aspect of your health care, whether or not you appoint an agent. Choices are provided for you to express your wishes regarding the provision, withholding, or withdrawal of treatment to keep you alive, as well as the provision of pain relief. Space is also provided for you to add to the choices you have made or for you to write out any additional wishes. If you are satisfied to allow your agent to determine what is best for you in making end-of-life decisions, you need not fill out Part 2 of this form.

Part 3 of this form lets you express an intention to donate your bodily organs and tissues following your death. Part 4 of this form lets you designate a physician to have primary responsibility for your health care.

After completing this form, sign and date the form at the end. The form must be signed by two qualified witnesses or acknowledged before a notary public. Give a copy of the signed and completed form to your physician, to any other health care providers you may have, to any health care institution at which you are receiving care, and to any health care agents you have named. You should talk to the person you have named as agent to make sure that he or she understands your wishes and is willing to take the responsibility. You have the right to revoke this advance health care directive or replace this form at any time.

Part 1: Power of Attorney for Health Care

(1)   Designation of Agent: I _____ , of

_____ ,

California, designate the following individual as my agent to make health care decisions for me:

_____
Name of Individual You Choose as Agent

_____
Address

_____
City   State   Zip Code

_____
Home Phone   Work Phone

First Alternate Agent (Optional): If I revoke my agent's authority or if my agent is not willing, able, or reasonably available to make a health care decision for me, I designate as my first alternate agent:

_____
Name of Individual You Choose as First Alternate Agent

_____
Address

_____
City   State   Zip Code

_____
Home Phone   Work Phone

Second Alternate Agent (Optional): If I revoke the authority of my agent and first alternate agent or if neither is willing, able, or reasonably available to make a health care decision for me, I designate as my second alternate agent:

_____
Name of Individual You Choose as Second Alternate Agent

_____
Address

_____
City   State   Zip Code

_____
Home Phone   Work Phone

(2)   Agent's Authority: My agent is authorized to make all health care decisions for me, including decisions to provide, withhold, or withdraw artificial nutrition and hydration and all other forms of health care to keep me alive, except as I state here:

_____

_____

_____

_____

_____
Add Additional Sheets If Needed

(3) **When Agent's Authority Becomes Effective:** My agent's authority becomes effective when my primary physician determines that I am unable to make my own health care decisions unless I mark the following box. If I mark this box ☐, my agent's authority to make health care decisions for me takes effect immediately.

(4) **Agent's Obligation:** My agent shall make health care decisions for me in accordance with this power of attorney for health care, any instructions I give in Part 2 of this form, and my other wishes to the extent known to my agent. To the extent my wishes are unknown, my agent shall make health care decisions for me in accordance with what my agent determines to be in my best interest. In determining my best interest, my agent shall consider my personal values to the extent known to my agent.

(5) **Agent's Postdeath Authority:** My agent is authorized to make anatomical gifts, authorize an autopsy, and direct disposition of my remains, except as I state here or in Part 3 of this form:

_____

_____

_____

_____

_____

_____

_____

_____

_____

_____

_____

_____

Add Additional Sheets If Needed

(6) **Nomination of Conservator:** If a conservator of my person needs to be appointed for me by a court, I nominate the agent designated in this form. If that agent is not willing, able, or reasonably available to act as conservator, I nominate the alternate agents whom I have named, in the order designated.

Part 2: Instructions for Health Care

If you fill out this part of the form, you may strike any wording you do not want.

(7) **End-of-Life Decisions:** I direct that my health care providers and others involved in my care provide, withhold, or withdraw treatment in accordance with the choice I have marked below:

☐ (a) Choice Not to Prolong Life
I do not want my life to be prolonged if (1) I have an incurable and irreversible condition that will result in my death within a relatively short time, (2) I become unconscious and, to a reasonable degree of medical certainty, I will not regain consciousness, or (3) the likely risks and burdens of treatment would outweigh the expected benefits.

☐ (b) Choice to Prolong Life

I want my life to be prolonged as long as possible within the limits of generally accepted health care standards.

(8) Relief From Pain: Except as I state in the following space, I direct that treatment for alleviation of pain or discomfort be provided at all times, even if it hastens my death:

_____

_____

_____

_____

_____

_____

_____

Add Additional Sheets If Needed

(9) Other Wishes: (If you do not agree with any of the optional choices above and wish to write your own, or if you wish to add to the instructions you have given above, you may do so here.) I direct that:

_____

_____

_____

_____

_____

_____

_____

_____

Add Additional Sheets If Needed

Part 3: Donation of Organs at Death

(10) Wishes for Organ Donation: Upon my death (mark applicable box):

☐ (a) I give any needed organs, tissues, or parts.

☐ (b) I give the following organs, tissues, or parts only:

_____

_____

_____

_____

_____

_____

_____

Add Additional Sheets If Needed

☐ (c) My gift is for the following purposes (strike any of the following you do not want):

    (1) Transplant

    (2) Therapy

    (3) Research

    (4) Education

Part 4: Primary Physician

(11) Designation of Primary Physician: I designate the following physician as my primary physician:

_____
Name of Physician

_____
Address

_____
City   State   Zip Code

_____
Phone

Secondary Designation: If the physician I have designated above is not willing, able, or reasonably available to act as my primary physician, I designate the following physician as my primary physician:

_____
Name of Physician

_____
Address

_____
City   State   Zip Code

_____
Phone

Part 5: Signatures

(12) Effect of Copy: A copy of this form has the same effect as the original.

(13) Signature: Sign and date the form here:

    Dated: _____

_____
Sign Your Name

_____
Print Your Name

Alternative #1: Witnesses

(14) Statement of Witnesses: I declare under penalty of perjury under the laws of California (1) that the individual who signed or acknowledged this advance health care directive is personally known to me, or that the individual's identity was proven to me by convincing evidence, (2) that the individual signed or acknowledged this advance directive in my presence, (3) that the individual appears to be of sound mind and under no duress, fraud, or undue influence, (4) that I am not a person appointed as agent by this advance directive, and (5) that I am not the individual's health care provider, an employee of the individual's health care provider, the operator of a community care facility, an employee of an operator of a community care facility, the operator of a residential care facility for the elderly, nor an employee of an operator of a residential care facility for the elderly.

First Witness

_____
Signature of Witness

_____
Print Name

_____
Address

_____
Date

Second Witness

_____
Signature of Witness

_____
Print Name

_____
Address

_____
Date

(15) Additional Statement of Witnesses: One of the above witnesses must also sign the following declaration:

I further declare under penalty of perjury under the laws of California that I am not related to the individual executing this advance health care directive by blood, marriage, or adoption, and to the best of my knowledge, I am not entitled to any part of the individual's estate upon his or her death under a will now existing or by operation of law.

_____
Signature of Witness

Alternative #2: Notarization

Certificate of Acknowledgment of Notary Public

State of California

County of _____ } ss

On _____, _____, before me, _____ ,

personally appeared _____ ,

personally known to me (or proved on the basis of satisfactory evidence) to be the person whose name is subscribed to the within instrument, and acknowledged to me that he or she executed the same in his or her authorized capacity and that by his or her signature on the instrument, the person, or the entity upon behalf of which the person acted, executed the instrument.

WITNESS my hand and official seal.

_____

Notary Public for the State of California

[NOTARY SEAL]   My commission expires _____

(16) SPECIAL WITNESS REQUIREMENT: The following statement is required only if you are a patient in a skilled nursing facility—a health care facility that provides skilled nursing care and supportive care to patients whose primary need is for availability of skilled nursing care on an extended basis. The patient advocate or ombudsman must sign the following statement:

Statement of Patient Advocate or Ombudsman

I declare under penalty of perjury under the laws of California that I am a patient advocate or ombudsman as designated by the State Department of Aging and that I am serving as a witness as required by Section 4675 of the Probate Code.

_____
Signature of Patient Advocate or Ombudsman

_____
Print Name

_____
Address

_____
Date

Cut →

Attention: Emergency Medical Personnel

I _____

[insert your name] of _____

_____ *[insert your address]*

have prepared an advance health care directive stating the
type of medical care I wish to receive if I am incapacitated
and unable to speak for myself. I have also appointed a
health care agent to oversee my wishes. In the event of a
medical emergency, please contact one of the people listed
on the reverse of this card, in the order listed.

©Nolo 2003   [OVER]

Fold →

[insert the location of an easy-to-find copy of your directive]
_____

My advance directive for health care is located: _____

[insert your doctor's name and phone number]
_____

My Primary Physician: _____

_____

My Alternate Agent: _____

[insert agent's name and phone
numbers where agent can be reached in an emergency]
_____

My Agent: _____

Revocation of Advance Health Care Directive

I, _____ ,

of the City of _____ , County of _____ ,

State of California, revoke the advance health care directive dated _____ ,

empowering _____

to make health care decisions for me. I revoke and withdraw all power and authority granted

under that directive.

Dated: _____

_____
Signature of Principal

_____
Print Principal's Name

Do Not Resuscitate (DNR) Order

I, _____ ,
direct that if my heart stops beating or if I stop breathing, no medical procedures be initiated to resuscitate me, including chest compressions, assisted ventilations, intubation, defibrillation, or cardiotonic medications.

I hereby agree to and request this Do Not Resuscitate (DNR) order.

If the principal's health care agent or other medical surrogate is signing this form on behalf of the principal, by signing this form, the surrogate acknowledges that this request to forgo resuscitative measures is consistent with the known desires of, and with the best interest of, the individual who is the subject of the form.

Dated: _____

_____
Signature of Principal

_____
Print Principal's Name

_____
Principal's Address and Phone Number

_____

_____

Dated: _____

_____
Signature of Physician

_____
Print Physician's Name

_____
Physician's Address and Phone Number

_____

_____

Uniform Statutory Form Power of Attorney
California Probate Code Section 4402

NOTICE: THE POWERS GRANTED BY THIS DOCUMENT ARE BROAD AND SWEEPING. THEY ARE EXPLAINED IN THE UNIFORM STATUTORY FORM POWER OF ATTORNEY ACT (CALIFORNIA PROBATE CODE SECTIONS 4400-4465). IF YOU HAVE ANY QUESTIONS ABOUT THESE POWERS, OBTAIN COMPETENT LEGAL ADVICE. THIS DOCUMENT DOES NOT AUTHORIZE ANYONE TO MAKE MEDICAL AND OTHER HEALTH CARE DECISIONS FOR YOU. YOU MAY REVOKE THIS POWER OF ATTORNEY IF YOU LATER WISH TO DO SO.

I _____ ,
   Your Name and Address

appoint _____ ,
       Name and Address of the Person Appointed, or of Each Person Appointed If You Want to Designate
       More Than One

as my agent (attorney-in-fact) to act for me in any lawful way with respect to the following initialed subjects:

TO GRANT ALL OF THE FOLLOWING POWERS, INITIAL THE LINE IN FRONT OF (N) AND IGNORE THE LINES IN FRONT OF THE OTHER POWERS.

TO GRANT ONE OR MORE, BUT FEWER THAN ALL OF THE FOLLOWING POWERS, INITIAL THE LINE IN FRONT OF EACH POWER YOU ARE GRANTING.

TO WITHHOLD A POWER, DO NOT INITIAL THE LINE IN FRONT OF IT. YOU MAY, BUT NEED NOT, CROSS OUT EACH POWER WITHHELD.

INITIALS

_____ (A) Real property transactions.

_____ (B) Tangible personal property transactions.

_____ (C) Stock and bond transactions.

_____ (D) Commodity and option transactions.

_____ (E) Banking and other financial institution transactions.

_____ (F) Business operating transactions.

_____ (G) Insurance and annuity transactions.

_____ (H) Estate, trust, and other beneficiary transactions.

_____ (I) Claims and litigation.

_____ (J) Personal and family maintenance.

_____ (K) Benefits from Social Security, Medicare, Medicaid, or other governmental programs, or civil or military service.

_____ (L) Retirement plan transactions.

_____ (M) Tax matters.

_____ (N) ALL OF THE POWERS LISTED ABOVE.

YOU NEED NOT INITIAL ANY OTHER LINES IF YOU INITIAL LINE (N).

Special Instructions

ON THE FOLLOWING LINES YOU MAY GIVE SPECIAL INSTRUCTION LIMITING OR EXTENDING THE POWERS GRANTED TO YOUR AGENT.

_____

_____

_____

_____

_____

_____

_____

_____

_____

_____

_____

_____

_____

_____

_____

_____

_____

_____

UNLESS YOU DIRECT OTHERWISE ABOVE, THIS POWER OF ATTORNEY IS EFFECTIVE IMMEDIATELY AND WILL CONTINUE UNTIL IT IS REVOKED.

This power of attorney will continue to be effective even though I become incapacitated.

STRIKE THE PRECEDING SENTENCE IF YOU DO NOT WANT THIS POWER OF ATTORNEY TO CONTINUE IF YOU BECOME INCAPACITATED.

EXERCISE OF POWER OF ATTORNEY WHERE MORE THAN ONE AGENT DESIGNATED:

If I have designated more than one agent, the agents are to act _____ .

IF YOU APPOINTED MORE THAN ONE AGENT AND YOU WANT EACH AGENT TO BE ABLE TO ACT ALONE WITHOUT THE OTHER AGENT JOINING, WRITE THE WORD "SEPARATELY" IN THE BLANK SPACE ABOVE. IF YOU DO NOT INSERT ANY WORD IN THE BLANK SPACE, OR IF YOU INSERT THE WORD "JOINTLY," THEN ALL OF YOUR AGENTS MUST ACT OR SIGN TOGETHER.

I agree that any third party who receives a copy of this document may act under it. Revocation of the power of attorney is not effective as to a third party until the third party has actual knowledge of the revocation. I agree to indemnify the third party for any claims that arise against the third party because of reliance on this power of attorney.

Signed this _____ day of _____ , 20 _____

_____
Your Signature

_____
Your Social Security Number

State of California, County of _____

BY ACCEPTING OR ACTING UNDER THE APPOINTMENT, THE AGENT ASSUMES THE FIDUCIARY AND OTHER LEGAL RESPONSIBILITIES OF AN AGENT.

Certificate of Acknowledgment of Notary Public

State of California

County of _____ } ss

On _____ , _____ , before me, _____ ,
personally appeared _____ ,
personally known to me (or proved on the basis of satisfactory evidence) to be the person whose name is subscribed to the within instrument, and acknowledged to me that he or she executed the same in his or her authorized capacity and that by his or her signature on the instrument, the person, or the entity upon behalf of which the person acted, executed the instrument.

WITNESS my hand and official seal.

_____

Notary Public for the State of California

[NOTARY SEAL]   My commission expires _____

Physician's Determination of Incapacity

I, _____,

of the City of _____, County of _____,

State of California, declare under penalty of perjury that:

1. I am a physician licensed to practice in the state of California.

2. I examined _____

   on _____, _____. It is my professional opinion that

   _____

   is currently incapacitated and unable to manage his/her finances and property.

Dated: _____

_____
Signature of Physician

_____, Physician

Certificate of Acknowledgment of Notary Public

State of California

County of _____ } ss

On _____, _____, before me, _____,

personally appeared _____,

personally known to me (or proved on the basis of satisfactory evidence) to be the person whose name is
subscribed to the within instrument, and acknowledged to me that he or she executed the same in his or her
authorized capacity and that by his or her signature on the instrument, the person, or the entity upon behalf
of which the person acted, executed the instrument.

WITNESS my hand and official seal.

_____
Notary Public for the State of California

[NOTARY SEAL]   My commission expires _____

RECORDING REQUESTED BY

AND WHEN RECORDED MAIL TO

_____

_____

_____

Revocation of Durable Power of Attorney for Finances

I, _____ ,

of the City of _____ , County of _____ ,

State of California, revoke the power of attorney dated _____ , empowering

_____

to act as my agent. I revoke and withdraw all power and authority granted under that power of attorney.

That power of attorney was recorded on _____ , _____ , in Book

_____ , at Page _____ of the Official Records, County of _____ ,

State of California.

Dated: _____

_____
Signature of Principal

_____ , Principal

Certificate of Acknowlegment of Notary Public

State of California

County of _____ } ss

On _____ , _____ , before me, _____ ,

personally appeared _____ ,

personally known to me (or proved on the basis of satisfactory evidence) to be the person whose name is
subscribed to the within instrument, and acknowledged to me that he or she executed the same in his or her
authorized capacity and that by his or her signature on the instrument, the person, or the entity upon behalf
of which the person acted, executed the instrument.

WITNESS my hand and official seal.

_____
Notary Public for the State of California

[NOTARY SEAL]   My commission expires _____

Revocation of Durable
Power of Attorney for Finances: Recorded   Page 1 of 1

Revocation of Durable Power of Attorney for Finances

I, _____ ,

of the City of _____ , County of _____ ,

State of California, revoke the power of attorney dated _____ , empowering

_____

to act as my agent. I revoke and withdraw all power and authority granted under that power of attorney.

Dated: _____

_____

Signature of Principal

_____ , Principal

Certificate of Acknowlegment of Notary Public

State of California

County of _____ } ss

On _____ , _____ , before me, _____ ,

personally appeared _____ ,

personally known to me (or proved on the basis of satisfactory evidence) to be the person whose name is
subscribed to the within instrument, and acknowledged to me that he or she executed the same in his or her
authorized capacity and that by his or her signature on the instrument, the person, or the entity upon behalf
of which the person acted, executed the instrument.

WITNESS my hand and official seal.

_____

Notary Public for the State of California

[NOTARY SEAL]   My commission expires _____

Index

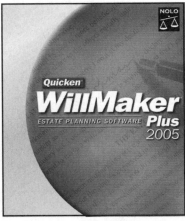

Remember:

Little publishers have big ears.
We really listen to you.

Take 2 Minutes & Give Us Your 2 cents

Your comments make a big difference in the development and revision of Nolo books and software. Please take a few minutes and register your Nolo product—and your comments—with us. Not only will your input make a difference, you'll receive special offers available only to registered owners of Nolo products on our newest books and software. Register now by:

PHONE
1-800-728-3555

FAX
1-800-645-0895

EMAIL
cs@nolo.com

or **MAIL** us
this registration card

fold here

Registration Card

NAME _____ DATE _____

ADDRESS _____

_____

CITY _____ STATE _____ ZIP _____

PHONE _____ E-MAIL _____

WHERE DID YOU HEAR ABOUT THIS PRODUCT? _____

WHERE DID YOU PURCHASE THIS PRODUCT? _____

DID YOU CONSULT A LAWYER? (PLEASE CIRCLE ONE)   YES   NO   NOT APPLICABLE

DID YOU FIND THIS BOOK HELPFUL?   (VERY)   5   4   3   2   I   (NOT AT ALL)

COMMENTS _____

_____

_____

WAS IT EASY TO USE?   (VERY EASY)   5   4   3   2   I   (VERY DIFFICULT)

We occasionally make our mailing list available to carefully selected companies whose products may be of interest to you.

❏   If you do not wish to receive mailings from these companies, please check this box.

❏   You can quote me in future Nolo promotional materials.
      Daytime phone number _____.

CPOA 2.0

Nolo *in the* NEWS

"Nolo helps lay people perform legal tasks without the aid—or fees—of lawyers."

—USA TODAY

Nolo books are ..."written in plain language, free of legal mumbo jumbo, and spiced with witty personal observations."*

—ASSOCIATED PRESS

"...Nolo publications...guide people simply through the how, when, where and why of law."

—WASHINGTON POST

"Increasingly, people who are not lawyers are performing tasks usually regarded as legal work... And consumers, using books like Nolo's, do routine legal work themselves."

—NEW YORK TIMES

"...All of [Nolo's] books are easy-to-understand, are updated regularly, provide pull-out forms...and are often quite moving in their sense of compassion for the struggles of the lay reader."

—SAN FRANCISCO CHRONICLE

fold here

Nolo
950 Parker Street
Berkeley, CA 94710-9867

Attn: CPOA 2.0